Transcendence

of

the

Western

Mind

Book and cover design and layout by
Martha Nichols/aMuse Productions

compari

ISBN: 0-9741976-0-2

Transcendence

of the

Western

Mind

Physics,
Metaphysics,
and
Life on Earth

Samuel Avery
2003

Contents

Chapter 1

The Structure of Consciousness

ALL IS BEFORE US. WHAT WE SEE IS WHAT IS REAL, AND THERE IS NOTHING unseen. Seeing is the universe itself. We touch and hear and think everything that is, directly and through each other. We are one consciousness. The difference between you and me is the structure of consciousness.

THE STRUCTURE OF CONSCIOUSNESS IS THE ANSWER. BUT WHAT IS THE QUESTION? Why do we need a structure of consciousness, and why is the Western understanding of the world inadequate to ask the question, or to answer it?

There are two questions to the answer. The first is, Why do space and time shrink and curve and blend into each another? The second is, How will we live when the oil is gone? These are vital questions. Space and time really do shrink and curve, and we really will run out of oil. But they are unrelated. I will, however, relate them. I will answer both questions with the same answer: the structure of consciousness. But my answer, though I have just called it one, is not really an answer at all. If you understand parts of what I have to say, you may think it an answer, but if you understand its wholeness, you will see that it is not an answer, only a better understanding of the question. This is how I hope you will come to appreciate what I have to say. We do not learn from answers, only from questions, and there are things we need to learn now.

Consciousness is wholeness, and being without separation. But there are parts, and a structure uniting them. Each part exists only in relation to the others. As multicellular beings, we are the composite experience of billions of cells, and as a complex society, the composite experience of the billions of us. But we are more than the sum of our cells, and more than the sum of

1

our separate selves. There is a quality of multicellular consciousness that no single cell can experience, and a quality of collective consciousness beyond the mind of any single person. This wholeness, this "suchness" that is being beyond its parts, arises from the particular structure through which the parts are interrelated. Let us look, then, at the parts, and then at the whole.

There are five realms of perception: touching, smelling, tasting, hearing, and seeing. Together they are perceptual consciousness as a whole. There are also nonperceptual realms. There is the realm of thinking, which we experience in the form of images and relations that we do not see or hear or touch; there is the realm of collective consciousness, which we experience in the form of information; and there is dreaming, imagination, and religious experience. Some of these are what we call "subjective" and some "objective," but they are all actual experience, and therefore "real," for my purposes here. Reality is conscious experience of any kind, not experience "of" something, but experience itself.

We think of consciousness arising from and reacting to an external world. We think of it as shaped and conditioned by external dimensional structures rather than as having a structure of its own. We imagine it inside a preexisting world, inside of ourselves and our brains, and capable of only partial appreciation of what is "really there," on the outside. We consider it an imperfect impression of the real physical world. But this is only how we think of it. We do not know what it is. Some think of consciousness as a soul inhabiting the body, or as a mysterious fluid condensed in the brain. Others understand it as a complexity of neural function arising at some indeterminate level of biological evolution. But I think that it is impossible to objectify consciousness in any way. I do not think we will ever be able to point to a lobe or cortex or gland or swarm of electrons and say, "This is consciousness." Identifying areas within the brain where specific neural functions take place is increasingly possible with advances in neurological science, but I do not think we will ever locate the being of consciousness at any place in the brain, or anywhere else. I do not think it has a location. I do not know what consciousness is any more than anyone else, but I am sure that it is not in anything or anywhere, or even at anytime. I think that the concepts of "in" and "where" and "when" are within it. I think that consciousness is everything. It is being itself. We will never find everything within anything. Consciousness is all of life, and the world is in it.

The structure that we see imposed on the world is more fundamental than the world itself. Space and time, rather than structures of the world that consciousness is in, are the means by which parts of consciousness are related to each other. They are the structures that connect the parts. Through space and time vision is related to touch, hearing to taste and smell. Through space and time the five realms of perceptual consciousness are related as a whole to collective consciousness. Dimensions are the means by which what I see is related to what I touch and hear, and also related to what I hear you say that you see. I see something *where and when* I hear it or touch it, and you tell me that you see and hear and touch it there, too. The structure of consciousness I am proposing is, therefore, a dimensional structure.

This is an understanding of life that transcends matter. More important, it transcends the difference between what you are and what I am. It is a transcendence of the Western understanding of reality. But there is nothing Eastern about it other than its initial approach. It is not Buddhist or Hindu, but it begins where they do, with the reality of experience foremost. It does not begin with a world and then try to figure out how life evolved within it; it begins with life and then tries to figure out where the world came from. I am suggesting it as an alternative to the traditional Western understanding of the world because the Western tradition has, through its pursuit of scientific truth, undermined its own materialist foundation. The more scientists have looked for the basic building blocks of the material world, the more they have found that they are not there.

My initial approach is through meditation. A long time ago I learned to practice meditation from a Buddhist monk, but the meditation I practice is not especially Buddhist, and I would not make a good Buddhist in any case. I am too interested in the world. When asked his philosophy of life, the Buddha would say that philosophy is not important. What is important is understanding how to transcend the cycle of death and rebirth. The world, he would say, is a distraction from the important business of attaining enlightenment. It is like an arrow in your back. If you are walking in the woods one day and you suddenly discover that someone has shot you with an arrow you do not go around asking what type of arrow it is, or who shot it, or what is the nature of the forest you are in; you try to get the arrow out. The rest is not important. But I am interested in the arrow. It is in my back and I cannot get it out. It is a beautiful arrow, and though I will eventually die of it, it fascinates me. The woods, too, are beautiful, when I can see them through the pain, and I will take time to say something about them as I lie here wounded. And though I cannot see him, I think I know who shot the arrow.

For me, meditation may or may not be a means of liberation, but it is a means of understanding. It is the means by which I have had a glimpse of consciousness as a whole and come to understand its parts in their relation. I have not received any special revelation, only taken the trouble to look at what anyone can see. Meditation, for me, is looking at life — just looking, looking without thinking or presupposing or categorizing or system building. Looking past what I think is true, drinking directly from the stream of life, without a cup. Even the structure of consciousness, though I think it is true, is something I try not to think about when I am meditating. I often see it anyway, and see parts of it I did not see before. Later, as I try to express what I have seen, I am usually disappointed with how my words sound in relation to the experience they attempt to represent. Things once clear and plain become tangled in ideas and concepts that mean other things, and seem too much my idea and not my vision. They sound too much like my thinking, which is what I am trying to get past. It is very difficult to filter what I see through the thinking self while trying to keep the self from getting in the way of what I say. It is a tricky business, and I cannot have succeeded completely. But if there is any validity to what I am presenting, it will be in what others see directly, without interpretation. It will be in what they see, and not what I say. And I hope that they will see not only more than I say, but more than I have seen.

I try to express what I have seen without reference to any particular tradition or method of meditation, and I avoid belief systems of any kind. You do not have to believe anything that you do not see. I try to avoid language specific to the study of religion, philosophy, or physics. If you do not meditate and do not have a Ph.D. in philosophy or physics, what I say should still make sense to you. But I invite you to give meditation a try for a minute or two, and to give physics a try, too, because I think that it is too important to be left to the physicists. You can understand what I have to say without either meditation or physics, but you will see it better with a little of each.

CONSCIOUSNESS IS STRUCTURED *DIMENSIONALLY* IN THAT EVERY PERCEPTUAL REALM is related to every other perceptual realm through space and time. Where and when I see something is also where and when I hear or smell it.

But the relation among realms exists whether or not there is *actual* perception in a particular realm. Even if I see an object and do *not* hear or smell it, the realms of hearing and smelling remain dimensionally related. If I hear or smell the object later on, it will be in the same location that I see it. In other words, consciousness is structured by *potential* perception. I see something where and when I potentially hear, smell, touch, and taste it. Dimensions are *sensory potentials*. This means that whether or not there is *actual* hearing where I see an object, there is always potential hearing at that location. This, and not material substance, is what constitutes a physical object. A physical object is a perceptual image that is actual in one or more realms but potential in all five.

If I see an object across the room that I do not actually touch, I know that I could touch it if I were to walk over to where it is. This is potential tactile perception. Because of potential tactile perception, I can touch what I want to touch and avoid touching what I do not want to touch. I can avoid being run over by trains and tractor trailers by perceiving through actual vision where and when there is potential tactile perception. I do not have to actually touch them. Similarly, I do not have to actually see or taste something if I smell it. If I smell something downstairs in the kitchen, I do not actually have to see a meal cooking to know that I could go and see it there, and taste it, too. This is potential visual and chemical (taste) perception.

Potential perception is really nothing at all. If unactualized, it is just empty space. If I do not actually see or touch or smell or taste or hear anything, all I experience is empty space, or pure nothingness. But potential perception, as nothing as it may be, is as important as actual perception. If there were no potential perception, we would not think about anything. We would not do anything. We only do things in order to actualize potential experience. We move across the room to actualize in the tactile realm what we see, or go down the stairs to actualize in the chemical realm what we smell. Potential perception is what we will see when we open our eyes or turn our heads, what we will hear or smell or taste when we go to the next room, and what we will feel when we reach out to pick something up off the table. It is the world that we are "in": the physical world. Potential perceptual consciousness is what we think of as "out there" waiting to be appreciated by us.

YOU MAY WONDER WHAT DIFFERENCE THIS MAKES. IS NOT POTENTIAL PERCEPtion really the same thing as the material world? Isn't it simpler to say that physical objects are made of a material substance that exists "out there" in space and time, whether we are looking or not? Why go to all the trouble of creating a new system to replace something that already makes sense? Who would ever know, in any case, whether we really experience dimensionally structured potential perception, or material substance?

On the everyday surface of things, in the normal workaday world, potential perception and the material world look and feel the same. If you wake up tomorrow morning and decide that matter does not exist but that your sensory realms are, instead, dimensionally coordinated with one another, you would notice no difference throughout the day. It is like the flat world that we live in on the everyday level of things. When you wake up in the morning, it does not matter whether the earth is really flat or round. You see the same things out the window, and walk the same way down the street. So long as you do not walk too far, there is no immediate practical difference between one way of looking at things or the other. The difference is only in how you understand things outside and beyond everyday life.

This brings us back to the two questions. Firstly, why do space and time shrink and curve and blend into each another? How can the nothingness of empty space be curved? What is it curved in? How can time pass more slowly in one place than in another? You would only know that these things happen if you were to walk pretty far away from everyday life. You would only know to ask the question if you had some exposure to what modern physics has been telling us about the way the world is. Space and time *really do* shrink and curve and disappear into each other, in places where things are very small, or very fast, or very large. This is not science fiction. We know this. It does not make sense in the world that we are used to, but we know that it is true. It even happens in the neighborhood where you live, but it is so small that you do not notice. It is even smaller than the curvature of the earth beneath your feet as you walk down the street. But it is there, and if you know it is there, you will begin to see a difference between the material world and the dimensional structure of consciousness. So I will try to tell you a little of what I know about modern physics.

If you are a physicist, or any kind of scientist, you may not be satisfied with what I have to say because it is not a theory. It is not provable or disprovable, which all theories have to be. Science does not deal in subjective experience, and I do. Science wants to know what everybody can experience, not what only one person experiences. To be provable or disprovable, a theory has to be objective — that is, you and I and everyone else has to see more or less the same thing and agree that it is true. But I do not believe there is a such thing as "objective experience," as we normally think of it. I will be saying that what we call "objective experience" is a special structure of what we call subjective experience and that they are fundamentally the same thing. It is true that there is a realm of consciousness that everybody can experience, but it is part of reality and not the whole. I go beyond the bounds of science and try to understand it as part of a larger reality that is not measurable and not itself dimensional. That is why I cannot submit this idea to scientific scrutiny. It is, I think, bigger than science. It explains an area that science itself has begun to explore but will never explain.

If it is not provable and not a theory, what is it? I will answer with another question: If the existence of matter is not provable, and therefore not a theory, what is it? Matter, though it cannot be proven to exist, plays an enormous role in how we understand who we are and what we are doing on Earth. I will put my idea, therefore, on the same level as the idea of material substance, and claim that neither is ultimately provable, but that my idea works better in view of modern physics. Whatever place matter now holds in our understanding of the meaning of life, that is the place I want for consciousness, and, more particularly, a dimensional structure of consciousness.

This brings me to the second question. We will learn to live without oil and other fossil fuels only when we know what they are.

Chapter 2

Being versus Doing

WHEN WE GET UP IN THE MORNING WE THINK OF THINGS TO DO, AND WE DO things all day long. This is the world we live *in*: the world of tables and chairs and getting to work on time. Doing is where we spend our time. We think of it as the world itself, with little pieces of being scattered through it.

BEING IS PURE BELIEF. IT IS BELIEF THAT NEEDS NO LOGIC. IT IS WHAT ACTUALLY IS AND cannot not be believed. Being is wholeness. Logical belief is an extension of being that creates wholeness from parts.

Being is thought and touch. It is seeing in your mind, and feeling on the side of your arm and beneath your feet. It is the sound of rain on wet ground and the vision in your eyes of the place where you are. It is the feeling you have in the roof of your mouth and at the back of your throat. It is the light of white sky that you see in late autumn beyond dark branches. It is remembrance of leaves. It is the smell of leaves now fallen and the thought of fallen leaves and how they smell. It is thumping in your chest that you hear in your ears when you stop to watch water dripping down the bark of trees. It is breathing in and out. It is cold on your hand as you touch the wet bark and smell water running through its dark furrows to the ground. It is a wet sleeve. It is a sadness you feel of summer past, and a hope for rest in winter. It is the thought of a dry place, and the awareness of a thought of a dry place. It is the thought that there is a dry place, and that you could go to it.

Being is the smell of leaves but not the leaves. It is the light but not the branches. It is the sadness but not the summer. It is the thought of being dry but not the dryness that is not. Being is everything that there is but not everything. It is perception but not its object. Being is actual experience: here, and only now. There are no other places and no other times. There are no possibilities, no things out of hearing or around the corner. Only this. Only what you see. Nothing other than what you see could be, only the thought, now, that there could be something else. That also is this.

Being is not a point in time and space. It does not move from past through present to future. It is now always. It is not in anything larger than itself. There is no there and then with being in it. There and then are now. The past is memory now. The future is possibility now. Down the stairs and around the corner is what I do not see. My friends in far-off cities are voices on the phone. The automobile a block away is a sound in my ear. There is no here there and no now then.

Being is the universe. There is nothing that it is not. It is the chair against my body and the sight of a table across the room. It is the bark of the dog. It is the light of stars and planets and faint galaxies at the edge of creation. It is what I see and think of. It is joy and sorrow, peace and anger. It is what I do all the time, yet I spend very little time doing it. I spend little time being because being is not in the time that I spend. Being does not fit in time. I cannot pin it down and say, "Now I will be for a few minutes." It does not work. I cannot find being in time because time is in it. It is like trying to find a haystack in a needle.

Being is all the time because time stretches across and covers being to its farthest reaches. Time lays on top of it, thinning only at the edges. Only at the edges can I, while I am I, see around time. Otherwise there is seeing through time, but I cannot be there when I do it. I, while I am I, can think of time only as something fundamental — something God made first and put everything else in. I cannot see thoughts and images coming through time and into images of time, but that is what they do. I do not see time emerging, even now. Unlike being, I am in the time that I am looking through. I am a fish knowing water without knowing what wet is.

It is my self that is in time that does the doing. Self moves through time and space and does more than be. Self comes with possibilities and choices and discontent. With it comes with nonbeing. It creates whole new potential worlds that are real but not actual, whole universes that could be but are not. Perpendicular to the actual world of space and time, they stretch infinitely in directions that are not space or time. I experience them. I do not touch them, but I need them to do things. I can do nothing with only the actual world. I look at them, not in space, but can do only one of the many things in them, and make it actual. I choose from an infinity of possibilities and bring it into space and time. The universe of "self-doing" is infinitely larger, therefore, than being, but within it and smaller.

KNOWING THIS IS ESSENTIAL TO HUMAN EXISTENCE. THAT DOING IS LARGER THAN but within being is critical to everyday life in that the relation between them is critical to our continuation of either. There is something we have gotten wrong about the relation between being and doing that we need to get right, and soon. Doing has gotten way out in front of being. My purpose here is to put it back into being.

In our time the material world, the world of doing, is dominant. We think of imagination as a pale copy of what is real. We think of the spiritual as subordinate to the material: an ephemeral, questionable possibility that does not fit in the dimensional world. We do not know what consciousness is or where it is, but think of it as *in* space and time. We think of life as a complicated material process within the anatomy. I suggest the opposite: The material world is an emanation of the spiritual. Physical reality is an aspect of consciousness. Yet what I say is based on physical evidence, and I will produce that evidence. Being is not something you do; doing is something that is.

This is important because we no longer know what it means to be human in relation to other forms of life at a time when humanity is engulfing other forms of life, and itself, in a technological progression that is out of control. The concept of matter is, I believe, at the bottom of how people relate to the rest of creation and to themselves. Because it can be manipulated by the human mind, and the human hand, matter has led us to look at creation almost exclusively in terms of doing. We derive our origins from matter and give it authority over us. It has become for us the sole reality. Where it once broadened our minds and opened a new world to us, it now narrows our vision and keeps us from seeing what is happening. Material substance is a myth that we should now outgrow.

Consciousness is another word for being. We usually associate consciousness with "self," which, I think, is incorrect. We think of a living organism as "having" consciousness, of consciousness being "in" it, and think of our own consciousness as something in ourselves. We think of "I" seeing rather than "seeing." It is these associations with self that keep the word *consciousness* from being the same thing as being. It is a good word otherwise, but it will be difficult to think of it in the way I mean to use it.

Consciousness as being means that all things are aspects of consciousness. There are no things outside of conscious experience: no tables and chairs sitting in the room waiting for you to turn around and look at them. It is not that they are there one minute and gone the next so much as that their reality is your experience of them. If there is no experience, there is no chair. Matter does not exist on its own. There is no physical world "out there." Conscious experience is the ultimate reality.

This conflicts with common sense, and very few people believe it. I believe it only because it is the simplest and best way to understand what we now know of physical reality. It is easier to understand atoms and quasars and black holes and quarks if we do not try to think of them as composed of a material substance separate from consciousness. It is just easier. Matter gets in the way. We do not need it, so we should get rid of it.

The reason we do not need matter is that the world works well without it. We do not need matter to see and touch things, and we will not notice if it is gone. We have never seen or touched matter in any case. We have never seen or touched anything outside of seeing and touching. We may think that we are touching an object that is already in space before we touch it, but that is just what we think. There has never been a way to prove that it is "really there" without our touching it. We may touch it at the same place in space and time that we see it and think that the coordination of touching and seeing proves that it is already there, but this may have to do with what space and time are. It does not prove matter. So if we get rid of the concept of matter we are getting rid of only a concept. Only our thinking will change; the world will remain the same. But it is very difficult to change thinking, and it should not be done lightly. It should only be done in the face of overwhelming evidence.

Being can make this kind of change. Being puts the parts into a whole and becomes the wholeness greater than the parts. Belief is a transitional process.

Being is the actual reality of perception, thought, emotion, communication and everything else that we experience exactly as it is. It is pure consciousness and there is nothing that it is not. Doing requires being, but also nonbeing. It requires the physical world as it is, but also the world as it might be when you are through doing something to it. It consists of objects as they *are* perceived in space and time and also as they *might be* perceived in space and time. It consists, therefore, not only of actual perceptual consciousness but of *potential* perceptual consciousness. We see and hear and touch things where and when they are, but we have to think of them being somewhere else in order to *do* something. The thought that leads to doing is like another dimension added to the physical world. It is not a dimension *in* the physical world, but one superimposed on the physical world. And it is not really a dimension, only *like* a dimension. It is an additional infinity of possibilities at a "right angle" to space–time, but we cannot measure it in meters and seconds the way we can space and time. If it is a dimension at all, it is not the same kind of dimension that they are. It is more accurate to say that there is a structure of consciousness, more fundamental than space or time, that shows up in the form of space and time, and also in the form of "thought that can be done" or, more plainly, "order." The *order* that you think but do not perceive before you do something is like a dimension. This is a fundamental structure of consciousness that underlies both what we perceive and what we do.

THE DIFFERENCE BETWEEN THE GENERALLY ACCEPTED VIEW OF PHYSICAL REALITY and what I am proposing is that I do not start out with a space–time "box" and put matter and consciousness inside it. I start out with consciousness and put the box in it. I keep the box, and accept the reality of the physical world, but say that space and time do not exist *absolutely* — that is, on their own. They need us. I do this not because it makes us more important (which it does), but because space and time work better this way. I am not trying to make us more important than we thought, but we are.

I will try to show that mass also works as a dimension the same way space and time do. It works better as a dimension than "order" in that it is measurable like space and time. Grams add and subtract the way meters and seconds add and subtract. Grams mix with meters and seconds to make momentum and force and energy the way meters and seconds mix to form velocity and acceleration. Mass works considerably better as a dimension than as a quantity of material substance when it comes to quantum mechanics and relativity theory, and also when it comes to understanding something as simple as inertia in everyday experience. It interacts with space and time the way space and time interact with each other at *dimensional extremes*, or at extremely large or small distances, velocities, and gravitational fields.

With the inclusion of mass, there are five physical dimensions: three of space, one of time, and one of mass. There are also five perceptual realms of consciousness: seeing, hearing, smelling, tasting, and touching. This may be a coincidence, but it has led me to suspect a relation between physical dimensions and realms of consciousness. I call it the principle of dimensional correspondence. It is a guess that makes sense out of the confusion surrounding modern physical science. Everything else I say here is based on it. If it is wrong, the whole idea is wrong.

Dimensional correspondence is an alternative way of tying together seeing, touching, hearing, smelling, tasting, and the order that accompanies doing. These realms of consciousness have been tied together in the past by the supposed existence of material substance external to consciousness: They were together "out there" in the box before they were perceived or thought of, and that is why I see a pencil on the desk at the same place and time that I feel it. But I am saying now that separate realms of experience are tied together by a structure that is within consciousness itself. I am saying that I see the pencil *where* I touch it because that is what space is. Space is what coordinates separate realms of perception. To know what I am getting at, try to experience your visual realm by itself. Don't think of it as in your head or in a room or at some location in a universe. Just look at what you are actually experiencing. Images are sharp and highly defined in the middle and fuzzier around the edges. The field of vision itself seems to have a circular or oval shape, but it is not a shape *in* anything. There is no space outside of the edges of the field. When an object near the edges attracts your attention, you move the field of vision as a whole so that it is centered on the object. You are not moving the field in space; you are moving space in the field. You are "scrolling" space through your vision so as to place the object of attention in the center, where it can be viewed clearly. This scrolling through space makes it seem that you are moving in space. It is like watching television where the screen is your field of vision and you control the camera.

But you cannot smell or taste objects you see on television. A television screen has two dimensions of space and one of time, while your field of vision has three of space and one of time. Smell and taste and the other realms of perception each have their own separate "fields." How are they intercoordinated to produce one five-realm world instead of five one-realm worlds? Vision is tied to your field of hearing and taste and smell through these dimensions; that is why you hear things where you see them and see them where you taste them.

But touch is different. Touch requires an additional dimension that is not built into your field of vision at least in any immediate way. When you touch things, you feel an *acceleration* that can only be experienced as another time dimension "foreshortened" in space–time. You do not experience acceleration at any one point in space–time; you can only measure it through several related points. Acceleration "stacks up" in space–time more or less the way the third space dimension "stacks up" on a two-dimensional picture or photograph. (You can see acceleration in space–time the way you see depth in a two-dimensional picture of a three-dimensional object.) Physicists express acceleration in terms of meters per second *per second*. Your "field of touch," or the "tactile realm," is your body. When you touch things, you accelerate them, and they accelerate you back. When you move your body as a whole, you "feel" acceleration as a whole. You do not feel space–time; you feel space–time–time. You feel only the second time dimension. If you move at a constant velocity (without accelerating), you feel nothing.

By "scrolling" space in an orderly manner you can see things where you hear them and touch them where you smell them. I call this scrolling a "dimensional interchange," or a rotation of the axes of space and time and time–time within consciousness. It makes you look and feel like you are moving in space. Through dimensional interchange you can push things around that you see and touch, and change their arrangement in space and time. This is doing.

Doing is the whole universe through the perspective of "self," or just about everything that fits inside dimensions. But it does not include imagination, spirit, emotion, and what might be called nondoable thought. It does not include being, which is also everything. Being goes beyond dimensions. Being can exist without doing, but not doing without being. We often forget this as we go about things.

There are two advantages in tying together realms of consciousness in this way. First, physical science makes better sense, as I hope to show. This would be enough were we interested in a new worldview purely for its intellectual economy. Second, being is united. If we rely on matter to tie together realms of consciousness, being is divided into little pieces in me and in you and in every other living thing, and I do not think we can keep living this way for much longer. Being will have to be united, and doing will have to be done within being, if we are to do anything about the way things are going.

SOME OF YOU READING THIS BOOK MAY BE INTRIGUED BY WHAT IS SAID HERE BUT intimidated by black holes and space–time and relativity theory. Others may have trouble with realms and potentials and Eastern philosophy. I hope I have not lost you already. But it is impossible to say what I have to say without these because physics is the science of what is, and Eastern philosophy provides the best initial approach, I believe, to understanding what physics says about what is. To make a case for the structure of consciousness that is behind black holes and relativity theory, as well as behind everyday life, I must indulge in what will seem convoluted language. It cannot be avoided. But I have tried hard to make the language understandable to those willing to understand it, and can only hope that you are able to see through the words to what they describe. In any case, it is not a better understanding of physics, or philosophy, that is my goal, but a better understanding of the world that has produced them.

Chapter 3

American Meditation

MEDITATION IS POSSIBLE IN AMERICA IN THE GEOGRAPHIC SENSE ONLY. IT IS A nothingness that must be explained as something, a hole through the culture that surrounds us and that tells us who we are. Meditation is not working or shopping, resting or playing, nor is it praying. It is not a part of anything familiar. It is like some forms of prayer, but it is not praying. It is not deep thinking, and it is not musing or imagining things. Few Americans know how to do it. It is, therefore, intriguing and new. It might be the answer to something. But it is not an answer, and it will disappoint anybody who thinks it is anything. It will disappoint anyone who tries to do it. This is true in America or anywhere else, but truer in America because we are more likely to be disappointed by the disappointment.

What happens when you try to meditate? You sit on the floor and try not to think about anything. But you are thinking about trying not to think, so you stop that. It starts again, and you realize that you have been thinking about not thinking about not thinking, and that is good because you can watch that. Before long your legs hurt and your back is aching, so you look at that. You congratulate yourself because you are meditating when you are able to watch the pain, and the thought of the pain, but you are not doing it when you congratulate yourself. You thought you were getting somewhere but the thought itself proves otherwise. Soon you are thinking about work, or picking up the kids, and your leg really hurts, and you give up. It is too much for you and you have failed again. What were you doing this for, anyway? It has taken time that you could have used raking leaves or fixing the gutter. You have told yourself you would do this every day, but tomorrow's out because there is a meeting to prepare for — an important meeting. Maybe you will continue later in the day, but you know how later in the day is likely to turn out.

What do you tell your friends you are doing? What happens when the phone rings? Your family might cover for you, but what do they tell their friends? You have to find a spot that is quiet and safe from accidental discovery. Bring a book with you, or the newspaper. Always be prepared to be doing something. If someone should find out the truth, be prepared to explain it as best you can. Be confident in who you are and what you believe in. But can you explain it to yourself? Isn't this a little self-indulgent? You could be doing volunteer work at the shelter.

In America there is nobody to tell you to go at it again the next day. And if there were, what would he say?

LOOK AT WHAT IS. LOOK AT THE LOOKING AT WHAT IS. DON'T TRY TO MAKE ANYthing happen. Most of the time nothing will happen. It is like learning to play tennis. You put on the shoes, you go to the place, you grunt and sweat and strain and chase a little green ball around, and most of the time you fail to do what you are trying to learn. Most of the time you do not hit the ball well. That is what makes it learning. Most of the time your attempt to meditate will not be what you hope.

So you need encouragement. Your tennis partner will do this for you. Your friends will understand what you are going through. But in America there are few to encourage you to meditate. And they will say things foreign to our culture. In America there is a different understanding of what life is and where it comes from. There is a different understanding of what thought is.

Occasionally you will experience something in meditation that is due to your having meditated. It may be a sense of calm: a deep peace, perhaps, or a feeling of having made sense of things. You may have a direct experience of being greater than yourself, and you may wonder if you have imagined it. You may discount it accordingly, or you may have learned to experience imagination as reality. In any case, you will feel good that you have accomplished something after so much work. But if you make it yours, it will not be what you are trying to do. You cannot use it as a place to go back to. You will never be able to go back to what you remember because your memory of it is not what it is. So accept the encouragement, if you like, but know that it is only a trick to keep you going. The wonder and the joy are as the pain and monotony. They are opposing aspects of the reality you are transcending and no more to be sought than avoided. Just look at them.

And on those rare occasions when you have experienced what is due to your having meditated, and your foot is asleep and your back can take it no longer and you are falling once again into the thought of self-doing, know that there is no understanding in America for what has happened to you. There is no allowance here for you to experience being anything other than yourself. It all happened within you. The human mind is capable of all sorts and kinds of imaginings, and we have a special science for that. It is our way of keeping some order.

In the West, reality is not the same thing as experience. Reality is what anyone, not just you, can experience at anytime. This reality is experienced only through symbols, be they linguistic or mathematical. You have to be able to put what you experience into words or numbers for other people to accept it as real. Eastern thought, generally, allows for the reality of direct experience, for what you experience and nobody else experiences — for thought, imagination, spirit, and consciousness itself. These things are real in themselves, not only in their reduction to neural processes. Where meditation in the West is often seen as looking "inward," at oneself (where consciousness is thought to be), in the East it is looking neither outward nor inward but at whatever is. "West" and "East" are gross generalizations as I use them here, of course, but where the metaphysic of the West tends to question the validity of meditation experience, that of the East accepts it.

Look at What Is

LOOK AT THE SOUNDS. LOOK AT THE THOUGHTS AND FEELINGS. LOOK AT THE fear and boredom. Look at the pain of sitting in one position for too long. There is always plenty to look at — too much, in fact. As these rise and fall, look at the breath. It is always there. Look at the heartbeat. Look at gravity at the bottom of your feet. Look at the thought of gravity at the bottom of your feet. Look at everything. Concentrate on one thing. Watch yourself trying to concentrate on one thing. Do not not look at something else. Watch your mind wander. There is nothing you can do about it.

Sit comfortably. Do not lie down. Or go ahead and lie down, but meditation will be more difficult. You can stand up, too. You can meditate while mowing the lawn. But you should be comfortable so that you will not have to do anything. Doing narrows consciousness to that which is done, and we are interested in seeing what is. Sooner or later you will have to do something, like move an arm, or turn your head, or shift your weight, and you will not see as much, but you may look at that, too. Sitting comfortably quiets the mind and allows it to expand beyond the doing and the doable. That is why you should sit comfortably. But if you try too hard to be comfortable, you will have to do something. You may start out comfortably, but you will always end up uncomfortable if you sit for more than a few minutes, which you should. You should sit long enough to become uncomfortable. Watch yourself become uncomfortable. Look at the desire to move a leg or scratch your nose. Watch the desire grow and overcome your will to remain still. Then go ahead and move — or scratch. Meditation is not a contest to see how long you can take it. Endurance is not the goal. But as soon as you move or scratch, the desire to move or scratch becomes the moving or scratching, and the desire itself, which you are looking at, becomes what is. Consciousness has contracted, and you are back in "self-doing." You will have to begin to meditate all over again. This will happen many times in each session, depending on how comfortable you can make yourself initially. Let it happen, and watch it. Do not try to make it not happen.

In the East, where meditation traditions are many thousands of years old, sitting positions have evolved that help quiet the mind and minimize doing. There are many traditions and many positions. If you wish to learn meditation within a particular tradition, you should learn the positions and practices that it teaches. But do not be surprised if the position is uncomfortable, perhaps extremely so — at least at first. Your first few sessions, or even your first few years of sessions, may revolve around mindfulness of pain within your legs and back. This may be exactly what you need, or it may be too much for you and turn you away from meditation entirely. I think it is a bad way to start. The endurance of pain is not what meditation is about. After extended practice one may find that pain may be experienced without reacting to it, but this is not the same thing as endurance. The transcendence of pain is a sure sign that the mind has been calmed, but it is not a good goal to set when beginning the practice of meditation. In any case, it is likely that sitting on the floor without furniture is considerably more difficult, and painful, for the modern Westerner than it was for those who developed meditation postures in the East a thousand or two years ago. They were used to sitting on the ground, and you are not. You may have to sit in a chair. But do not get hung up on procedure. The tools are important, but they are not the job at hand.

Sit comfortably and look at what is. Watch your mind trying to sit comfortably and trying to look at what is. Why can you not do it?

Remove the Labels

MANY PEOPLE ARE DISAPPOINTED THAT NOTHING HAPPENS WHEN THEY MEDITATE. They sit and listen to the traffic and the neighbors talking next door and think about parking tickets and lawn mowers and dental appointments. They are unable to do what they have set out to do. Nothing happens. There are no voices from within, no inspirations, no glimpses of nirvana. The world does not melt into an ethereal blissfulness. There is only the same old stuff. Many times when you are meditating you will just see the same old stuff. You will think, Nothing new here.

But it is *all* new. Everything you experience is entirely new — and different. The pressure on your left elbow, the sound of the airplane in the distance, and the thought of your friend in the store yesterday afternoon are all new. Absolutely new. You have never experienced them before, and never will again. What are not new are the labels: "friend," "airplane," "elbow." When you feel the pressure of your foot on the floor, you put a label on it and file it away with other, similar feelings. This helps you make sense of what you are experiencing, but it also makes you stop paying attention to it. As soon as you know "what" a sound or a tactile sensation is, you stop experiencing it as it is. Almost every experience can be labeled, and that is why nothing new ever seems to happen. If there is a scream in the night, or a UFO appears outside your window you may run short on labels and begin to pay attention. That is what meditation is about. You pull the labels off and pay attention to the most commonplace experiences. In meditation you pay attention to life itself. That is what distinguishes it as meditation.

Chaos

WHAT IF YOU WERE ABLE TO REMOVE ALL THE LABELS? WHAT WOULD IT LOOK like? You would hear a car passing on the street, but you would not think "car" or "street." You would hear someone talking in the next room, but you would not think "someone" or "talking" or "English" and you would hear only the sounds of the words and not think their meaning. If you were able to see past these labels there would be other, more fundamental labels beneath them. There would be feelings and thoughts and sounds, but you would have to see them without thinking "feeling," "thought," "sound." Without these labels there would be no way to distinguish between one type of experience and another. You would have nowhere to file what you saw. Would you experience the difference between "feeling" and "hearing"? Is the difference in what you experience, or only in how you categorize it? Is the difference in the label? Is the label there, in the experience, or something you add on? Are "you" a label?

If you were able to remove all the labels, you would not be able to make sense of what you saw. It would be pure chaos.

Look at the chaos. Watch it tumble and boil and spit out thoughts and things and pieces of scenery. It is there, always, and you can see it, but only in bumps and glimpses. And you cannot remember what you saw. You remember only labels. You remember only "chaos," not chaos. You see only chaos now, and not in time, because time is a category in which you put experience, and not experience itself. Chaos is not in time. If you see chaos you do not remember it. And you are not you when you see it.

When you are trying to see chaos the labels always come back. Little labels like "toe," "elbow," and "bird," and big labels like "room," "me," "time to go eat lunch." The labels arise from the chaos. The chaos is consciousness, and the labels are the world.

But what have I said here? "Chaos is consciousness, and the labels are the world." This is a very radical thing to say, and I have slipped it by you when you were not paying attention. It undermines what we take for granted in the West. In the West it is not true that the world arises from consciousness because consciousness and self are more or less the same thing. How can the world arise within self? Whose self does it arise in? The question risks a very ugly answer. If the world is in me, you are in me, and you have no consciousness of your own. This is what we must think in the West if the world arises from within consciousness, so we do not think it. We think that there are many selves, each with its own consciousness, arising within the world. This works if you do not look too deeply into the chaos. Or if, strange to say, you do not know about modern physics.

Meditation does not fit well in Western culture because there is not very much to look at inside your self. The world is outside, in the towns and the streets and in the media, and that is where things are happening. To look inside your own skin is to see your skin from the inside. This may be interesting, for a time, but limiting, and ultimately self-indulgent. It is blocking out the world, which is so much bigger than one person. Meditation is understood in the West as a form of introspection, a way of examining faith and morals and options, and of reviewing one's own thoughts and motivations, but it is not generally understood as a way to know about the world.

Look Past Self

NOW LOOK AGAIN AT WHAT IS. FOLLOW THE BREATHING, OR RECITE YOUR mantra, or do whatever you do to calm the mind. As always, do not try to make anything happen. This time, try to hear what you are hearing and feel what you are feeling without thinking "I" hear this, or "I" feel that. Just listen to the sound itself. Feel the feeling without the feeler. You cannot stop the "I" from arising, but you can watch it arise. It does not have to be there. It wants to be there, but it does not have to be. It will be hard to see past it because it is very strong, as strong as you are, and it will want to be there at least as much as you want it not there. Even the wanting of it not to be there is what it is.

The self arises from being in order to create doing. When you feel a pain in your lower leg, the self wants to move it somewhere else, and thoughts arise as to where and how to move it and why you should really do it right now instead of waiting until you said you would stop meditating. The self is not satisfied just looking at the pain, and this is why it is so difficult to look past self. This is why it is so difficult to be without doing, and why when you do it you cannot do it at all.

But you can do it. Do not try to make it happen; let it happen. Do not even let it happen; just watch what is happening. There is a place that is breathing in and breathing out; breathing in and breathing out, and you may watch it anytime. It is not you breathing in and breathing out, but it is the only one that you will see. The mind will want to grab it and say "It is only me, breathing," but forget about that. Let it grab and release. The mind will tire of grabbing, but the breathing will continue.

Remember that there is nothing in it for you.

You have to quit sometime and do something. It never fails.

When you become aware of not meditating you have reached a point where you no longer need a reason to meditate.

The arrow is in my back.

The arrow is in my back. I want to know what it is and how it got there. I am not so anxious to pull it out as I should be, for it is suffering, but also love and joy. It will mean my death, but I have yet the rest of life, I think. I will pause and tell you what I see before I try to pull myself from it, if I ever get it out. It is interesting, and I think you will enjoy hearing about it. It is all I have.

We do not feel space. Nor do we feel space–time. What we feel is space–time–*time*, or acceleration. Steady motion has no feeling whatsoever. Gravity on the surface of the earth is a fixed position in a curved space–time. What we feel in our bodies is a constant acceleration upward against the downward "pull" of a curved space–time. space–time is curved into space–time–time. So we feel space–time–time even when we are not moving. (If there were no gravity we would not.)

But space, and the notion of accelerating "through" space, is derived from visual, and not tactile, perception. We see things rushing past us that we do not feel. Space comes from vision. We would have no notion of being any-where in particular, or of going anywhere, with tactile consciousness alone. The difficulty of understanding the idea of being "at rest" on the earth's surface, while feeling acceleration, is the difficulty of reconciling the tactile and visual realms. On the surface of the earth we are at rest in space–time (which is why it does not look like we are going anywhere), but not at rest in space–time–time (which is why we feel gravity). Einstein figured this out in his "Principle of Equivalence" between gravity and acceleration. They are the same thing. They feel the same. They only look different.

The connection between tactile and visual consciousness is the "photon." It has a dual nature: It is both felt and seen. It is the smallest unit of visual consciousness, and a single point of energy in space, time, and mass. Nothing smaller can be seen, no matter how powerful the microscope, because the space in which it is seen does not get any smaller. The photon produces the space that it is in. It is like a dot in a newspaper photograph. The picture arises from a spatial arrangement of many dots, and can be no smaller than a single dot. But as a unit of energy, a single photon can be felt as well as seen. It can be either a particle or a wave. Individual cells "feel" individual photons. That, in fact, is what I think a photon is. It is the experience of an individual retinal cell as reported to the organism as a whole. The cell feels; the organism sees.

A photon is not what an individual cell experiences; it is what an individual cell experiences as reported to the body as a whole. Individual retinal cells have their own lives that the organism as a whole knows nothing about. The photon is just the part they tell us about. It is just a dot they pass on to a picture they do not see. Cells don't need space because they know only about their own dot, and nothing about how it is arranged with others. But the dot is meaningful because it is in a context that the organism as a whole can understand, an informational configuration we know as space. It thereby becomes distinct from other tactile sensations, and "filed" in a category of experience distinct from the tactile realm — "seeing." But the picture produced by photons for the organism as a whole has to coordinate with three other categories of perceptual information — hearing, tasting, and smelling — for a total of five categories. As a unit of energy, the photon is a five-dimensional entity. Its location in three dimensions of space, one of time, and one of frequency (per time) gives it the capacity to relay information in five entirely separate, but coordinated, realms of experience.

IN THE WEST WE THINK OF GRAVITY AS A FUNCTION OF MATTER. IT IS MATTER that "pulls" other matter, or "curves space–time." Matter is at the bottom of everything. It is what "matters." Matter is our ultimate reality. We may choose to believe other realities, but they can leap only so high before matter pulls them back. They fall back to its hard surface always. Matter defines and confines the experience of being. What we see and hear and think is in reaction to what is before and after we see and hear, and beyond what we think. Matter is the primal stuff of life, and experience is a dim and fleeting glimpse of the material, and an approximation only. Being is so very, very small, and the world so very large and indifferent.

Meditation is an idealistic attempt to escape the gravitational field of matter, and it has never been known to succeed. There are physical laws to prevent it. It is a looking within the brain, within the body, within the world, a forced watching of the mind arranging and rearranging its understanding of external objects. Interesting, but unproductive. If you watch someone in the act of meditation you will not see him do anything. He will sit for a while, rise, and walk away. If you try it yourself, you will sit for a while, rise, and walk away.

LOOK AT WHAT IS. LOOK AT THE RISING AND FALLING OF THE BREATH, AND OF thoughts. Look at looking and at feeling and hearing. Do not concern yourself with anything *about* what you see. Do not associate it with anything else, if you can help it. Do not think of "me seeing," just see. Do not think of the sound "in the next room," just listen to it as it is. You may watch thoughts sorting themselves into images of feeling or seeing, and thence into this or that object of feeling or seeing, and you will lose yourself in this, and become yourself, but always come back to looking at what is. You will never go wrong in this. Whenever you do not understand and wish to see what is directly, look at what is — directly. You will still not understand, but you will see.

It is always accessible and rarely found.
It does not speak yet you may see words closing in around it.
It is beyond any concept of God.
It is the source from which God issues Godself, and It.

The labels are the world as I see it, but what about the world that I do not see? How is the larger world constructed from the seeing, hearing, and thinking of one person in one place?

If you have practiced some meditation, you have noticed that there are many different kinds of labels. The most fundamental of these separate experience into seeing, hearing, smelling, touching, tasting, and thinking. These six categories are well defined and highly structured, but not altogether absolute or comprehensive. We will not say that all experience must fall into one of these, nor that there is no crossover among them. Emotions, for instance, may constitute a separate fundamental category, or they may be said to overlap two or three of the others. We will not try to create watertight definitions in any case, but we will say that there is a very definite structure at the level of sensory realms. "Below" this level consciousness is undifferentiated; "above" it there are at least six distinct realms of consciousness that are easily identified.

Five of these are sensory, or perceptual, realms. What distinguishes perceptual realms from undifferentiated consciousness is that what we experience in them implies a world much larger than their actual content. When I hear a sound I sense that there is not only the hearing itself, but also an object making the sound, *and* a world that the object is in. Where did the object and the world come from? This is at the heart of the difference between Eastern and Western thought. It is also at the heart of the metaphysical limitations of Western science.

The object and the world do not come from the hearing itself. When you hear a bark, you do not hear a furry, four-legged creature with floppy ears, and you do not hear the neighbor's yard behind the fence. You think these things, but you do not hear them. You think them because you have seen a four-legged creature make this sound, you have felt his fur, and you know by the direction the sound is coming from that what you have seen and touched before is behind the fence in the neighbor's yard. You associate the sound "bark" with a previous vision "four-legged" and touch "furry." You have previously seen the yard behind the fence, and envision the dog standing there barking. You do not actually experience a dog in the yard, but you assume that he is there, causing the sound of the bark, and that is why you hear it. You assume that there is an object, and a world. At the moment that you hear the bark, all you know is that there is a bark.

In the West you have to assume that there is a dog and a world because otherwise nothing would make sense. How else do you explain the fact that you saw a four-legged creature in the yard yesterday making the same sound? The simplest explanation for the apparent coordination of sensory perceptions is that there is a dog in the world causing barks and four-legged visions and furry sensations when you happen to be listening or looking or touching. The dog is there all the time, whether you are perceiving him or not. He exists outside of perceptual experience. The material substance that he is made of is more fundamental than consciousness. You have no way of experiencing the dog except through consciousness, but you have to say that he is there all the same. It is a belief that has to be there to hold the world together. And it is a pretty good belief. No matter how you test it, it works.

Let us say that you hear the bark but are not convinced that there really is a dog "out there" in the world. So you get up and go out the back door and look over the fence. There he is or, to be more precise, you experience there a visual perception of a four-legged creature at the same place that the bark is coming from. Strictly speaking, there is still no "dog in the world," only a visual four-legged creature and an auditory bark that are coordinated in space. There is no proof of a material dog, but the assumption is holding up well. There is certainly no disproof. To be safe, you take it a step farther. You climb over the fence and reach your hand out to the same point in space where you see the four-legged creature and hear the bark. You feel a furry sensation exactly at that point. Still no proof of a dog outside consciousness, but the tactile realm of perception appears to be dimensionally coordinated with the visual and auditory. The best and simplest explanation is that there is a world outside of consciousness causing this dimensional coordination of perceptual experience. In fact, why not say that the world *is* the dimensional coordination? The dimensions are there all the time: We and our separate consciousnesses are in them along with an array of material objects that interact with each other and that we experience when we are looking. This is what we assume in the West. We may not think it through, but we assume it, and it works.

It works if you do not look too closely. Most people most of the time will continue to assume that they are in a material world and never know the difference. But we are reaching a point now where the limitations of the material world are showing. We cannot long live in it.

LET US GO BACK, THEN, TO WHAT IS. UNDIFFERENTIATED CONSCIOUSNESS CHURNS and waves through the mind and falls under the labels "seeing," "hearing," "thinking," etc. How is it possible to construct the world from labels alone? When you hear the "bark" you think "dog," even though you do not see the dog. But implicit in the *actual* hearing is *potential* seeing. You do not see the dog at that moment, but you know that if you look out the back window you will see him. As the experience "bark" falls under the category "hearing," a relation is established to the category "seeing," even though there is no actual seeing going on at the time. There is an underlying structural relation between "hearing" and "seeing" that lends enormous new meaning to whatever is heard. "Seeing" and "hearing" are not just loose categories independently floating about in the mind, but highly structured realms of perception that create a sense of "world" from sounds and sights. The relation is one between the categories themselves, and not between the actual sounds and sights that fall into them. What is heard is not what is seen. The fact that it is "hearing," however, means that there is potential "seeing." The bark does not tell you what the dog looks like, only that you will see something if you look in the same place that you hear the bark.

The relation between hearing and seeing is space. You hear the bark coming from where you will see the four-legged creature when you look. Space is the potential within which actual hearing and seeing take place. It is also the potential for the other realms of perception: Where an object is seen or heard is also where it may be touched or smelled or tasted. All five perceptual realms are coordinated in space. Actual perception in any realm is always structurally related to potential perception in every other realm. This is how sounds or smells or tastes become physical objects, and why objects appear to exist above and beyond consciousness. Space is a structural relation among perceptual realms that is more fundamental than anything within them.

IS THERE SUCH A THING AS MEDITATION? YOU MAY PRACTICE DAY AFTER DAY, hour after hour, and never get anywhere. You know what you are supposed to do: Follow your breath, recite your mantra, watch your thoughts before they wander. You may be very determined to do it, but as soon as you think "I am doing it!" you are doing it no longer. It is gone as soon as it exists, if it ever existed at all. You can never really do what you think you are supposed to do. In this sense, there is no such thing as meditation. You are wasting your time.

MEDITATION IS UNANSWERING QUESTIONS. WHAT IS A PERSON? WHAT IS A DAY? What is gravity? These are all questions that we have answered long ago for ourselves and for each other. But the answers have become labels that we no longer see past. What really is a "day?" We have never known what these things are, and we never will know what they are simply by giving them a name. To answer is to block the growth of awareness. We have too many answers and not enough questions. No wonder there is no wonder. Look through and past the thought structures by which you think you know things. Throw away the answers and look at the questions.

To do things we need answers. But if we are doing the wrong things we need questions. This is especially important for us now. What is humanity? What is weather? What is Earth? What are we supposed to do with ourselves here? These are questions that should be unanswered, and they should stay unanswered as long as possible. We have to do something else, something different with ourselves, but we should hold off the answers until we can hold them off no more. When we answer them finally, we will not be what we are now.

Chapter 4

The Myth of
Material Substance

WHEN YOU REACH OUT TO THE GLASS OF WATER ON THE TABLE IN FRONT OF you, your fingers touch it where your eyes see it. You assume that the glass is something other than your experience of seeing or touching, that it exists on its own, waiting in space, ready to be perceived at any time. How else to explain the coincidence of more than one perception at the same place and time? It was there before you looked at it, and would be there if you had chosen not to look in its direction. It is something "out there," a material thing, independent of consciousness, requiring no living being to be what it is. The matter of which it consists creates the connection between the seeing and the touching, and also the connection between *you* seeing it at the same time and place that *I* see it. Matter explains why you see the same glass again the next time you look. There has to be material substance in the world causing these coincidences.

But there is no proof. There is no way to verify the existence of material substance external to conscious perception; you cannot experience anything outside of experience. You can know that you see the glass on the table, and that you feel it as you pick it up, and that the seeing and touching occur at the same location in space and time, and you can also know that another person standing nearby would say that he sees and touches as you do. But you cannot say that the glass exists independently of the seeing and touching. You can assert the existence of a material glass as a logical necessity, arguing that it *must* exist, or there can be no order in the world, but there is no way for you to prove it directly. The glass, as something outside of consciousness, remains an argument, an opinion, a statement of faith in a reality that supports so much that we hold dear. A material glass has to be there to explain the world we have come to know.

Such is the role of myth. Myth explains what we know to be true. It creates a holistic picture of the world by filling in gaps between points of verifiable knowledge and by tying together loose strands of actual experience. Its source is the imagination — that uncreated part of consciousness beyond logic and perception, outside of space–time, and outside of all dimensionally related objects in the universe. Myth does not originate within perceptual experience, and cannot be verified within the realms of perceptual experience. It is not untruth, merely unprovable truth. It is not a lie, merely a fabrication; there is no deceit intended. Myth lends meaning to life, and thereby creates the world it lives in.

It cannot be my purpose, therefore, to destroy a myth in the name of truth and meaning. A myth — any myth — is always true in its context, always meaningful, and always necessary for life. It makes being understandable and doing possible. It can never be disproved for the same reason that it can never be proved. I cannot prove here or anywhere else that matter does not exist and will not try to do so. I can only show that there is something simpler, more beautiful, and more meaningful. I can only suggest that there is a better myth. Mythology, by virtue of its origins in unstructured consciousness, is a fluid and pliable thing, and subject to process and evolution. It can change — improve, even. It is not entirely random in its scope, as it must tie together what is known. It cannot ignore new knowledge. It must reshape itself continually in order to be meaningful, and thus to retain its right to be at all. Myth must change with time. As more becomes known, new meaning must be found and old meaning left behind. Whole new generations of mythological creatures arise and do battle with the Titans of the past, eventually to replace them as new worlds are born.

The myth of material substance, born some two thousand, five hundred years ago on the Ionian coast of ancient Greece and raised during the era of classical paganism, came of age under the guidance of Medieval Christianity. It has matured in the modern world and borne its fruit. It will live on, in diminished form, for centuries to come, but has no more to offer us now than what it has given already. It has run its course. A new mythology based on the meaning of new knowledge will take its place. In this way we will become something other than what we are, and survive what we have created.

THE EXISTENCE OF MATTER IS INTUITIVELY OBVIOUS. IT IS SO OBVIOUS THAT VERY few people have actively questioned it. Many who have considered the question in some depth recognize the unprovable nature of matter but, realizing that its nonexistence is also unprovable, conclude that the world makes better sense with than without it. It is better to believe in it by choice, as a matter of convenience. Matter thereby becomes a working hypothesis that gets us through the day, real or not. It works well most of the time. Until broken, do not fix it. If you do away with the concept of matter, many people feel you will end up with chaos, since the modern scientific worldview is built entirely on a material foundation. Without matter you have to base reality on thought, opinion, and other less reliable forms of experience that are subjective, inconsistent, and too weak to support the weight of a modern technological civilization. A world cannot be built on philosophy alone. Civilization is too valuable, most would say, to be undermined for the joy of metaphysical speculation.

But despite every argument for its continued existence, material substance remains hypothetical. The man who challenged it more systematically than any other modern Western thinker was George Berkeley (1685–1753), Bishop of Cloyne. Bishop Berkeley granted the reality of sensory experience, but not the reality of any sort of material substance connecting distinct perceptions within the various sensory realms:

> ... I see this *cherry*, I feel it, I taste it: and I am sure *nothing* cannot be seen, or felt, or tasted: it is therefore *real*. Take away the sensations of softness, moisture, redness, tartness, and you take away the *cherry*. Since it is not a being distinct from sensation; a *cherry*, I say, is nothing but a congeries of sensible impressions, or ideas perceived by various senses; which ideas are united into one thing (or have one name given them) by the mind; because they are observed to attend each other. Thus when the palate is affected with such a particular taste, the sight is affected with a red colour, the touch with roundness, softness, &c. Hence, when I see, and feel, and taste, in sundry certain manners, I am sure the *cherry* exists, or is real; its reality being in my opinion nothing abstracted from those sensations. But if by the word *cherry* you mean an unknown nature distinct from all those sensible qualities, and by its existence something distinct from its being perceived; then indeed I own, neither you, nor I, nor any one else can be sure it exists.[1]

In his dialogues between Hylas and Philonous, Berkeley seems to admit the impossibility of proving the nonexistence of matter, but claims that the burden of proof is on the believer, not the burden of disproof on the nonbeliever:

> (Hylas has just claimed that there are two kinds of objects: the one perceived immediately through the senses, and the other "real," or "material," which is not perceived through the sense, but through the "mediation of ideas," which are the images and representations of the real object.)

Philonous: I would therefore fain know, what arguments you can draw from reason for the existence of what you call *real things* or *material objects*; or whether you remember to have seen them formerly as they are in themselves; or if you have heard or read of any one that did.

Hylas: I see, Philonous, you are disposed to raillery; but that will never convince me.

Philonous: My aim is only to learn from you the way to come at the knowledge of *material beings*. Whatever we perceive, is perceived either immediately or mediately; by sense, or by reason and reflection. But as you have excluded sense, pray show me what reason you have to believe their existence; or what *medium* you can possibly make use of to prove it, either to mine or your own understanding.

Hylas: To deal ingenuously, Philonous, now I consider the point, I do not find I can give you any good reason for it. But thus much seems pretty plain, that it is at least possible such things may really exist; and as long as there is no absurdity in supposing them, I am resolved to believe as I did, til you bring good reasons to the contrary.

Philonous: What! is it come to this, that you only believe the existence of material objects, and that your belief is founded barely on the possibility of its being true? Then you will have me bring reasons against it: though another would think it reasonable, the proof should lie on him who holds the affirmative.[2]

Bishop Berkeley's insight is undeniable. He has found a fatal flaw in the metaphysical foundation of Western civilization. There are no answers to the questions he poses; no one has ever experienced matter in any direct way and never will. Why, then, do we hear so little about him? Why was he forced to spend the rest of his life defending the truth that he had discovered rather than developing it into a new metaphysic? Why was he and is he still considered little more than a sideshow in the Western philosophical tradition? Why did no one else take up his cause?

Berkeley's problem was timing. The early eighteenth century was no time to question a myth that was well entrenched, rising rapidly, and on its way to bearing its greatest fruits. The concept of matter was already well developed in his time and just beginning to uphold the weight of modern science. It was too essential at that time to be questioned.

A man with much better timing was Rene Descartes. Living the century before Berkeley (1596–1650), Descartes caught the wave of scientific materialism well before it crested. His greatest accomplishment was to establish the material universe as a separate, and by implication, paramount reality. He admitted the existence of a spiritual or mental reality, but the "substance" of the body and of the physical universe was to be considered entirely separate from the substance of the mind or spirit: "By substance, we can understand nothing else than a thing which so exists that it needs no other thing in order to exist." Matter was there, with or without mind, and mind, presumably, with or without matter. Each world was to be understood only on its own terms; there was to be no attempt to unite them in any causal manner. Descartes was a devoutly religious man, and avoided conflicts between the church and science by skillfully forcing them into entirely separate arenas.

But a connection between mind and body must exist. He attempted to explain it by placing the soul (what we would call "consciousness") inside the pineal gland, a small endocrine organ deep within the posterior forebrain. But by situating the spiritual world at a location *within* the physical, he established, wittingly or otherwise, a distinctly subordinate role for the mind vis-à-vis matter. Mental phenomena were supposed to fit in some way into the material world, and not the material world into the mind. The specific location suggested by Descartes has never been accepted by the modern world, but the suggestion that the soul, or mind, exists somewhere inside the body is universally accepted, or at least not questioned seriously. We generally agree that mental phenomena are separate from the physical world, but we attempt nonetheless to understand them as best we can in terms of physical processes in space and time.

Another indication of the primacy of the material over the mental in Descartes's world is his discussion of primary and secondary qualities of perception. Primary qualities are those of shape, number, extension, and mass. They exist objectively and absolutely, in the "real" world. Secondary qualities are color, taste, and odor, etc. They are subjective and ultimately unreal — little more than pale reflections of what is really there. The secondary qualities are not to be trusted because people experience the senses in different ways. I may think an apple tastes good, and looks dark red in a certain light, and you may think otherwise; the "real" apple is just there in space, reflecting light and releasing certain chemicals when bitten. If there is any discrepancy between what is experienced and what exists in the material world, the fault lies with the experience, or what is thought to have been experienced. Material substance is the source of all true experience; mental substance can only approximate the inherent perfection of material substance.

Descartes established the mythological foundations of the modern era by clearly delineating the material world and separating it from the world of the church. By separating that portion of human experience that could be well understood in terms of causal relations from that which could not, he set the groundwork by which human attention could be concentrated on those things which could be manipulated, changed, and built, or in other words, on that part of human experience that could be bent to human will — that is, on doing. A technological civilization requires a channeling of imagination toward what could exist but does not yet, and a bold confidence in the ability of human beings to make things exist that do not — exactly the view provided by a mythology based on material substance. Matter bends to human purpose. It exists on its own but has no life of its own. It is always out there, waiting to be seen, touched, heard, pushed, moved, shaped, and harnessed. There is nothing about its ultimate metaphysical nature or purpose that would keep people from doing whatever they wish with it. It has no inherent resistance to manipulation; any failure to shape or control it is failure not of matter itself, but of human knowledge and skill. It is lifeless, spiritless, and without purpose *until* manipulated by people. Unlike spiritual substance, man need not stand in awe of matter; he need not praise it, worship it, or consider its well-being. He need not *fear* it. He can do whatever he wants and it will not retaliate.

The material world is where things happen in the Cartesian mythology, and where man finds his purpose. The mental world exists in a sort of universe parallel to the material, but it is not where the action is. Causal relations and the power of manipulation do not extend far into the realm of the soul. Less can be understood, therefore, about the workings of the mind and less can be done about what is understood. What is actually "done" in the world of the mind is more a reflection of the material world than a world in its own right. Imagination is restricted to what might be called the "conditional material," or what might possibly exist in the material world. The rest is idleness. "Useful" thinking is not that which exists in its own right, but that which leads to successful manipulation of material objects. If we are to be productive people, we should spend our time thinking about better ways of doing things.

In this concentration of human attention on what can be done in the material world there is a narrowing of overall experience. Imagination devoid of practical application is not developed, and spiritual experience loses its meaning altogether. We do not know how to understand art, music, tales of miraculous events, mystical experiences, or mythology itself. Our minds are so focused on doing that we cannot relate to the vast experience of our pre-materialist ancestors. We are puzzled by the fact that *all* preliterate people *everywhere* lived their daily lives by fantastic stories of imaginary creatures that to us are patently fictional. How could they believe so deeply in what they never saw? We think of the imagination that was so much a part of their experience as childish, useless, and untruthful. How could they be so ignorant? Why did they never grow up? We do not understand them because the world we live in, while much more highly focused than theirs, is also much narrower. What we call fantasy was part of their world because it did not have to be doable to be real. They were capable of real experience outside of perception and "doable thought," and we are not.

This reduction in the overall scope of experience distorts the full picture of life and denies much of what is really experienced. It reduces reality. We still experience thought and imagination, and we still need spiritual experience, but we no longer consider it real. In this way much of what we live for becomes external to what we consider valuable.

Much is lost in this artificial confinement of conscious experience, but much is gained. The myth of material substance channels our sense of what is real and meaningful into a narrow stream of possibilities, but this keeps our minds on the task before us, as best we have been able to understand what that task is. We have learned with its guidance to concentrate on what we are doing, and we have done it well. It has helped us create a great new civilization.

That the Cartesian dualism between mind and body seems so obvious to us now indicates the extent of its influence. We have believed it for so long that it has become self-evident. To many, it is surprising that so fundamental a truth had to be invented by a human being. But Descartes' invention is no gratuitous construction. It is based on careful and systematic introspection and prolonged thinking and experimentation. His conclusions are clear and logical, and coincide closely with those of others of his generation and since. He did not invent the matter myth itself, only a means of delineating and expressing it. He merely put into words the prevailing thought patterns of his time, patterns that have since become the metaphysical foundation of modern civilization.

Like any myth, Descartes's is created in the imagination. He begins by doubting everything — God, religion, himself, the world, and matter — everything he has ever believed in — so as to clear the slate before filling it in again. He reduces experience to consciousness itself, attempting to go beyond mere belief in order to arrive at the basis of all truth. Myth is always deeper than belief to those who experience it directly. It is beyond logic and beyond self-evidence; it simply is because it is experienced. To those who do not experience the myth directly, it takes on the appearance of belief.

Having reduced reality to pure consciousness, Descartes resists the tendency toward logical construction by continuing to doubt whatever comes to mind. There is, therefore, in this most skeptical of worlds, nothing on which to build a metaphysic, until Descartes notices the doubting itself. *Something,* he concludes, must be doing the doubting. That something is, of course, himself. *He* must exist in order to doubt that he exists; "I think, therefore I am." Once this most fundamental of truths is established, he goes on, by means of logical process, to prove the existence of God, matter, Christianity, and all the angels. For Descartes, then, matter is not a given, but a conclusion based on the existence of self. Interestingly, he begins with consciousness and concludes with the existence of matter, but then puts consciousness back within matter!

It is unproductive, however, to criticize Descartes or anyone else for the illogic of their conclusions at this level of thought. Logic simply does not work until after fundamental truths are established. Conclusions reached at the foundations of experience are better evaluated in terms of their effectiveness: How well do they give guidance, meaning, and direction? How well do they work? There is no meaningful question as to their truth.

DESCARTES'S CONCLUSIONS HAVE WORKED BETTER THAN BERKELEY'S BECAUSE WE have needed them more. They have spoken to who we are and made it possible for us to do what we have done. But now, much later, there are quarks and black holes. Matter is condensed energy, which is not matter. Space and time curve around massive bodies. What happens to material particles on the quantum level depends on whether or not someone is watching.

And ozone, which used to be a molecule, is a life-giving presence that surrounds and protects us, requiring sacrifice.

Chapter 5

The Evidence
Against Matter

EVERYTHING REAL IS MADE OF MATTER. IT IS EVERYWHERE AND EVERYTHING IN THE universe; that is why we do not know what it is. As Descartes says, it is a substance that "needs no other thing in order to exist." But being everything, it cannot be much of anything. It can only sit there in space causing knowledge, itself unknowable.

Matter is where our thinking stops. If it is just there, without need of anything else, what is there to think of? The particular forms it takes fascinate us, but as a substance, there is nothing more to be said about it. It just is. If it were not, we would be looking into the dark.

THE RANDOM HOUSE DICTIONARY OF THE ENGLISH LANGUAGE, SECOND EDI-tion, gives three first definitions for *Matter*:

1. The substance or substances of which any physical object consists or is composed.
2. ... substance in general ... esp. as distinguished from incorporeal substance, as spirit or mind, or from qualities, actions, and the like.
3. Something that occupies space.

No surprises here. Matter is real stuff that is not motion, not appearance, and not mental. It is what is left when these are taken away. It is the only thing that we are absolutely sure is real.

We think of it as *hard*. In its most basic form it cannot yield to other matter. The space that it occupies cannot be occupied by anything else. When one billiard ball collides with another, the second must move out of the way.

Some physical objects, such as pillows, are not as hard as others, and may change shape when they undergo collisions. But it is the form of the object and not its matter that is soft. There is just as much matter in the pillow "fluffed out" as "pushed in." The substance within the pillow merely rearranges itself. Some objects are so soft as to allow the passage of other objects right through them. A cloud, for instance, can let an airplane fly through it without any apparent resistance. But the plane does not fly through matter; the matter of the cloud is in the millions of tiny water molecules that the plane pushes aside. The molecules are hard; the plane does not pass through *them*. The "cloud-ness" has no mass. The cloud, in fact, is somewhat suspect as an object; it is more of a *system* of material objects weakly interconnected by electrostatic forces. Matter does not care what objects or systems it is arranged into as long as it is given its own space to occupy.

Physicists have never experienced matter directly any more than the rest of us, but they detect its presence through *mass*. Mass is quantity of matter: An object's mass is the amount of matter that it has. Physicists can measure an object's mass anywhere in the universe in terms of its resistance to accelera-tion (inertia) when subjected to a known force. If you push an object with a lot of mass, it will not move as fast as if you use the same push on a less mas-sive object. More specifically, the heavy object will not *accelerate* as fast; it will not change its velocity as rapidly as the light one. Nobody knows how or why matter is able to resist acceleration, or why it is acceleration and not simple velocity that is resisted, or exactly what it is that matter is holding on to as it resists. But we know that mass resists acceleration so we can use it to detect and measure quantities of matter.

Before the twentieth century inertia was not so much a problem because most physicists, Newton included, believed that space was *absolute* — that is, that every point in the universe was fixed. Material objects simply cling to fixed space. When somebody tries to shove them, they stick their claws into space and hold back as best they can. But now most physicists think of space as *relative* — that is, having meaning only as a relation between objects. A chair is two feet from the table or ten feet from the wall, but nowhere in rela-tion to space itself. There are no fixed points in the universe that objects occupy or pass through. But if there is no fixed space anymore, to what do objects cling when they resist acceleration? What slows their motion when we push them, and how does this specifically relate to the amount of matter they contain?

We can detect matter through mass, but we can only measure mass through changes in motion. Definition number 2 above specifically distin-guishes matter from "actions."

The only other way physicists are able to determine the presence of matter is through gravity. In Newtonian terms, massive objects have a gravitational field around them that attracts other massive objects. Nobody at the time, including Newton, knew how this could be possible because it required "action at a distance." There is no apparent physical connection between the moon and the earth, yet they influence each other's motion and they do so instantaneously. Einstein's Theory of General Relativity does away with action at a distance by doing away with the idea of gravity as a force. Massive objects do not attract each other; they "curve" space–time in their vicinity. Objects moving in straight lines through this curved space–time only appear to be moving in curves. They are only apparently attracted by a force. Either way, gravitational fields are associated with massive objects and are an indication of the presence of matter. But we measure gravity in terms of acceleration. Again, we detect matter only in terms of "actions."

But if we put dictionaries and physicists aside for a minute, we will have to admit that even though we cannot measure matter without resorting to action, we can sense it through what we *feel*. We can feel matter, or at least mass. Objects with more matter are heavier: They are harder to lift or push. Even though we can measure mass only in terms of motion, we have a powerful intuitive sense that it is really there when we lift things. Anyone who doubts the existence of matter should unload a truckload of concrete blocks: He will *feel* their inertial resistance *and* their tendency to accelerate in a gravitational field.

But what is felt will be not matter, but mass. Mass can be felt directly. In fact, I hope to show that tactile perception is the source of our concept of mass. But the trouble with tactile perception is that it cannot be measured. In physics you have to be able to measure things or nobody is interested. Tactile perception is real — it exists every bit as much as auditory or visual perception — but there is no objective way to quantify it. It is what Descartes would call a secondary quality.

Mass can be measured in terms of meters and seconds, but only in a somewhat complicated form involving two time components. Simple velocity, or constant motion in a straight line, can be measured with a single time component — so many meters *per second*. You take an hour to drive 60 miles — that's sixty miles per hour. But mass, detectable through acceleration, can only be measured in terms of meters per second *per second*, or as the change in velocity over a given period of time. It takes several seconds after you step on the gas to get from 0 to 60. The more massive your car, the longer it will take. This is highly significant. Without this second time component (that I will later identify as a separate dimension), there would be no mass, and, interestingly, no tactile sensation. You cannot feel simple velocity. All you ever feel are *changes* in velocity.

BECAUSE WE MEASURE EVERYTHING WE IDENTIFY AS MATERIAL IN TERMS OF MASS, we do not need matter at all to do physics. Mass need not be a quantity of matter. It is something we feel, and something we can measure as a second time component of motion. This may not agree with the commonsense view of things, but it violates no laws of science. It may even help enforce a few.

But we have shown no reason that matter should not exist. If physics were only on the level of macroscopic objects (tables and chairs and other everyday things), we would do just as well to keep the concept of material substance. It explains things well and gives meaning to what we do. But the macroscopic physics that works on the everyday level cannot be extrapolated into the realms of the extremely large or the extremely small, or to the extremely fast or extremely massive. The physical concepts we use in everyday life do not work well, or at all, in dealing with distant galaxies, black holes, subatomic particles, and objects moving near the speed of light. These things are less common but just as real as tables and chairs, and must be accounted for if physical reality is to be understood.

The exploration of dimensional extremes began at the turn of the twentieth century. There was no systematic effort in this direction; scientists were beginning at that time to develop the instrumentation, and the curiosity, to look into things like atoms and distant galaxies. Before 1900 it was thought that the everyday world of tables and chairs extended infinitely in all directions in space and time. If you looked out at distant galaxies you would see bigger tables and chairs, and if you looked through microscopes you would see infinitely smaller and smaller tables and chairs. The universe was made of perfectly rectilinear (squared) space dimensions. Time was unconnected to space and passed evenly and smoothly at the same rate everywhere. The study of physics was the study of how matter moved within this universe. Consciousness played no part and was entirely unnecessary. The universe would go on its way whether anyone was looking or not. Physicists were so confident that they had answered the fundamental questions the world had to offer that some of them were a little worried that they would not have enough to do in the coming century. All that remained was to fill in a few gaps in the knowledge of how things worked and answer a few nagging questions about the nature of light. This is the universe that most people still live in.

But it was a universe too close to home. The real universe is much bigger. Galaxies beyond the Milky Way were not even known to exist at the turn of the century. The atom was an unproved hypothesis, and atomic structure was entirely unknown. Atoms, it was generally thought, would turn out to be tiny balls of matter chemically clumped together in various shapes and sizes and bouncing off one another like bumper cars. Light consisted of waves, much like sound waves, in some as yet undiscovered medium permeating the universe. Energy, momentum, pressure, force, acceleration, and velocity would be measurable in perfectly smooth, continuous, and infinitely divisible quantities of space, time, and mass. The accuracy of measurement was limited only by the accuracy of instrumentation. Bigger and better laboratories would provide bigger and better information within general outlines already established. Progress would be measurable in terms of decimal places. The secrets of life itself would one day be revealed as a complexity of physical process.

This world began to unravel in the year 1900 when Max Planck (1858–1947) discovered, to his own surprise and dismay, that energy does not exist in a perfectly continuous and divisible state, but comes in the form of tiny bundles, or "quanta." These quanta become apparent on the atomic and sub-atomic level. The energy of motion of an electron, for instance, is not smooth but "leaps" from one point to the next without ever occupying the space in between. Space, as we normally think of it, cannot be said to exist between the points that the electron occupies. Further study of "quantum mechanics" in the early years of the twentieth century showed that space, time, and mass become indistinguishable on the quantum level; the more you know about one, the less you can know about the others. Physicists found that there is a physical limit in our ability to locate "material" particles in space and time, and that this limit is built into the universe itself. No matter how big and powerful a microscope you have, you cannot say exactly where and when a particle is. Furthermore, the very act of observing these particles affects their behavior! "We," as conscious beings, are intimately connected with physical reality.

In 1905 Albert Einstein (1879–1955) discovered in his Special Theory of Relativity that objects traveling near the speed of light experience strange distortions in space, time, and mass. The faster they go, the shorter they get in the direction of their motion, the slower time passes, and the more massive they become! But no object can ever exceed the speed of light: There is something built into the fabric of the universe that keeps things from going faster than a certain number of meters in each second. And light, which imposes the speed limit, itself travels at the same speed *relative to everything*. If I am standing still and you are traveling past me at a million miles per hour, light will travel relative to both of us at the same rate!

These discoveries were not just curiosities. They showed that there was something very fundamentally wrong with our understanding of the universe as a "box" full of lifeless material objects and a few detached observers. We still cling to the box universe because it has always been home, but we are forced now to look more closely at just what the box is, and thereby, at what we are. We cannot ignore what we know.

I will try to describe, then, in very general terms, a few of the strange phenomena now confronting modern physical science. Some readers may find this tedious, but it is important that people who are not physicists take the responsibility to understand, in a general way, some of what is going on with the world that we all experience. It does not have to be a technical understanding. It does not have to involve mathematical symbols and you do not have to know the dialect. It is actually better, in some ways, to have a distance from the daily workings of physics if you are interested in the big picture. You can stand back and get a wider view. The exploration of the physical world is the special province of the physical science profession, but the understanding of that world is not.

Special Relativity

EINSTEIN'S THEORY OF SPECIAL RELATIVITY HAD MORE IMMEDIATE IMPACT THAN Planck's discovery. It grew out of a search in the late nineteenth century for a medium for the transmission of light waves. Light behaved very much like waves of sound or water, but nobody could find what was doing the waving. Sound consists of vibrating air molecules, and water waves of water molecules, but light waves did not seem to consist of anything at all. As this seemed impossible, it was hoped that an "ether," or medium for the transmission of light, would one day be discovered. Experiments were devised to detect the ether, but none of them were fruitful. Nobody could figure out why. For light to exist there had to be an ether of some sort that would fill all of creation, defining an absolute space relative to which all things moved, the sun and Earth included. The ether would provide a fixed universal grid work in relation to which all objects moved. If this were the case, light would move at a slightly different velocity relative to objects that were themselves moving. As the earth is a fairly rapidly moving object, its motion through the ether should be detectable. In its orbital path around the sun it should be moving in opposite directions through the ether at six-month intervals; with new instrumentation developed in the late 1800s it should have been possible to detect slight differences in the velocity of light measured every half year.

But the numbers did not add up. Despite numerous attempts with newer and better instruments, nobody was ever able to measure differences in light velocity, and thereby any relative motion of the earth through the ether. People who were working closely with the mathematics of light were finding that a fixed reference frame for light would not work well even in theory, especially for moving light sources. But it had to work, and the ether had to be discovered, because you cannot have waves of nothing. Einstein, who was not a physicist at the time, came up with the radical suggestion that nobody could find the ether because it did not exist. This was a shock. Light does not travel "through" any fixed substance, and its velocity does not change, even if its source is in motion. Light has no special or *fixed* frame of reference. It travels at the same velocity in relation to *everything*!

This agrees with experiment but conflicts with common sense. If two objects or observers are traveling at 90 percent of the velocity of light (c) in relation to each other, light travels at c in relation to *both* of them. How can that be? Normally, velocities add up: If you are driving by me at 100 miles per hour and shoot a bullet out in front of your car at 1,000 miles per hour, the bullet will be moving at 1,100 miles per hour relative to me. That is intuitively obvious and agrees with experimental findings. You would think, then, that if you turn on your headlights, the light coming from them would travel at c relative to you and at c plus 100 miles per hour relative to me. But it doesn't. It travels at c relative to both of us. This is the "constancy of the speed of light," and a primary principle of modern physical science. It is at the bottom of many other strange phenomena associated with relativity theory. Light appears to exist in relation to each individual observer, as if everybody has his or her own private space–time "box." As long as we remain at low velocities relative to one another, our "boxes" coincide; we can assume that there is only one box, and that we are all in it. It is only at extremely high velocities that our boxes begin to diverge.

If you and I are traveling past one another in rocket ships at, say, half the speed of light, each would see strange things going on in the *other's* ship (our ships being our "boxes," or "frames of reference"). Looking out my window, I would see everything on your ship *shorter* in the direction of motion than you see it. Your desk is a full meter long to you, but only 90 cm long to me. This is not an illusion. *Space itself* is shorter in your box than in mine, as I see it. To me, the meter stick you use to measure your desk is only 90 cm long when it is pointed in the direction of our relative motion. (As soon as you turn your meter stick sideways or up and down, it returns to a full 100 cm.) Time is also different for each of us. I see your clock running slower. For every full minute that I experience, I see you experiencing only 52 seconds! There is nothing wrong with your clock or mine: *Time itself* is passing slower for you from my standpoint.

Even stranger is that I see all of the objects on your rocket gain *mass.* Even as they grow shorter, they grow more massive! No additional material substance is pumped into them, but they behave as if it were, as if *mass itself* had increased uniformly through your entire frame of reference.

The gain in mass is proportional to the square of our relative velocity, as is the shortening of space and slowing of time. At half the speed of light the effect is noticeable, but not uncomfortably so. But as the velocity increases the effect increases exponentially. As it approaches the speed of light, the space dimension in the direction of motion approaches zero, time comes to a standstill, and mass becomes infinite. Full light velocity can never be reached, however, as no physical object can exist with a 0 space dimension at no time, and no force can accelerate an infinite mass the last meter per second to c. The speed of light is, therefore, a cosmic speed limit that applies to all physical objects in the universe. Nothing will ever go faster.

If space and time are absolute, how is it that they can be limited at all? How is it that the fundamental structures of the universe can be distorted *within* the universe? And how can light, which is supposedly "in" space–time, set the limits on how space and time are structured? But this is not all.

So far I have dealt only with what I see going on in your spaceship. What about what you see? You see nothing out of the ordinary in your own ship. Everything is normal: Your meter stick is a full meter long, even when you point it in the direction of our relative motion; your clock runs at a normal rate; and there are no changes in mass. As far you can tell, I am crazy to think there is anything out of the ordinary. But when you look in *my* ship you see what I saw in yours! My meter stick is 90 cm long, my clock runs slow, and everything in my box is more massive than it ought to be. Each of us sees the *same* effects in the *other's* frame of reference. You think I am crazy and I think you are.

Neither of us is right. I may think that you are moving and that I am at rest, and you may think that I am moving and you are at rest, but it doesn't matter. Since there is no such thing as absolute space, all velocities are relative, and there is no special or preferred frame of reference for the whole universe. Physical phenomena vary according to the velocity of the frame of reference, but there is no one box for everybody. Your box, my box, and everybody else's box are all different but physically equivalent, at least in terms of velocity.

But there is a way in which you and I are not equivalent. If you say my clock is running slow and I say yours is slow, what about total elapsed time? What happens when one of us slows down to the other's frame of reference and we compare notes? Total elapsed time will be different. Each of us saw the other's clock running slower, so we will have different ideas as to how long we were at separate velocities. One of us will have experienced more total time than the other, but which one? And how can there be an absolute difference in the time we experience if motion is purely relative?

The answer is that not all motion is relative. Only *constant velocity*, or "uniform," steady motion in a straight line, is relative. Bumps and curves and going to higher or lower speeds are all forms of acceleration. Acceleration is not relative. Positions in space and constant velocity are purely relative; but acceleration is absolute. If you were the one who experienced acceleration to half the speed of light and back, you will have experienced less total passage of time than I. You will claim that your interstellar vacation lasted for only a week, but you will have been gone from the office for a full month. On the brighter side, if you and I were the same age when you left, you will come back younger than I. You will feel the time passing perfectly normally in your "box," but the box itself, when accelerated, got out of step with mine.

But how, you may want to know, can acceleration be absolute if space is relative? Against what are you accelerating? There must be some sort of fixed frame "holding you back" as you move from rest to ½ c, or from 0 to 60 for that matter. How does your body *know* that it is accelerating? Science has no answer to this question. You could say it is due to the compacting of cells in your body, but there is no way to account for the compacting. How do *they* know they are accelerating? There is absolutely no way to explain the absolute nature of acceleration within the material worldview.

But your body knows that it is accelerating because it *feels* it. You feel a uniform kinesthetic sensation throughout your entire body as you *change* your velocity, whether increasing it, decreasing it, or changing its direction. This g force is the second *time* component of your motion, the second "per second." It is in direct proportion to the magnitude of your acceleration. If you accelerate rapidly, even for a short period of time — by swerving around a corner, jamming on the brakes, or going over a speed bump — it may be severe. If you accelerate slowly, you may barely notice it. But as soon as you level off to a constant velocity, even if it is half the speed of light, you will not feel it at all. You cannot feel space moving through you. What you feel when you *change* velocity is *space–time–time*. The acceleration you feel is motion in relation to the whole universe. Your falling out of step with the passage of time in my box is directly related to what you experience in the *tactile realm of perception*.

The high-velocity extreme of special relativity is where space, time, and mass distortions become noticeable, not where they exist. They exist at all velocities. Even observers passing by one another on the street have slightly different experiences of space, time, and mass. They are so close as to be negligible from the standpoint of measurement, but they are never exactly the same. The objective universe is never better than an extremely good approximation. In fact, what we call "normal" experience at relatively low velocities is a special case within a much larger context. It is normal only because it is familiar. Experiences at half the speed of light are every bit as real.

The same Theory of Special Relativity states the equivalence of mass and energy in the famous formula $E = mc^2$, where "E" is energy, "m" is mass, and c is the speed of light. This formula shows that "matter," or at least mass, can be used to fuel atomic bombs and nuclear power plants. But more interesting for our purposes is not that we can blow up cities and boil water with atoms, but that "matter" can become something else, and that the relation between mass and energy has to do, again, with the speed of light. How can a "substance" become heat and motion, and what does light have to do with the relation of atoms to energy? Why would the speed of light, much less the *square* of the speed of light, have anything to do with how mass is converted into heat and motion? What is it about light?

Einstein did not claim to know the answers to these questions. His job was to describe the new relations between space, time, and mass, not to interpret their metaphysical meaning. He continued to think of matter in space and time in more or less Cartesian terms, as do most physicists to this day. Myths do not change rapidly.

Physicists generally prefer the metaphysics they are brought up with because they do not care to unlearn so much of what they have assumed to be true. It is uncertain work, and beside the point of their everyday endeavors. Physicists do not like metaphysics because it is messy. There are too many opinions and too many pedagogical egos. You cannot measure things exactly and you cannot know things for sure. Metaphysical truth is a matter not of experiment but of argument, and there are no objective standards by which truths can be established and built on. But messy or not, the equivalence of mass and energy has a metaphysical meaning of far greater import than any physical meaning it will ever have. $E = mc^2$ is not just a recipe. It is not just a way of harnessing the atom to work for us. It is a fundamental statement of the relation between tactile and visual consciousness, and of how the world they create is structured. It speaks to what we are and what we are becoming. We will all live or die by how we understand it.

The equivalence of mass and energy is a question of being that we have answered only in terms of doing.

Distant Galaxies and Black Holes

ALL OF THE STARS THAT YOU SEE IN THE NIGHT SKY ARE IN OUR OWN MILKY WAY galaxy. Even the stars that you can see with the help of a small telescope are all in our galaxy. But you may also see with a telescope some small cloudy patches or "nebulae" scattering in among the stars. As late as 1900 nobody knew what these were. It was not known whether they were gas clouds fairly close to the earth, distant star clusters within the Milky Way, or separate galaxies altogether. Edwin Hubble (1889–1953) proved in the 1920s that at least some of them were separate galaxies at extreme distances from the earth. The known universe took an enormous leap in size.

But even more important was Hubble's discovery that distant galaxies were moving away from us at very high speeds, and that the more distant they were, the faster they were moving. The universe was expanding. But it was not just objects in the universe moving through space away from each other; it was objects more or less at rest in a space that was expanding. The box itself was exploding in all directions. At greater and greater extremes of distance, objects were found to be moving away from us, and from each other, at rates approaching the speed of light. Light from one of these objects is so "redshifted," or its wavelengths so spread out due to the receding motion, that it is barely recognizable as being from an "object" as such. It is hard to say whether we are getting light "from" a material thing billions of light-years away or just getting light.

The redshift of light from objects moving away from us is due to what is called the Doppler shift. This phenomenon is more usually experienced in the form of sound waves. Rapidly moving objects give off sound of a higher pitch as they approach and a lower pitch as they recede. This is because objects catch up with their own sound waves as they approach, shortening them and thus heightening the pitch, and then move away from their own sound waves as they recede, lengthening them and lowering the pitch. You hear this when a passing train blows its whistle. The high-pitched sound of the whistle as the train approaches drops suddenly as it speeds by. But the train has to be moving fast in order for the effect to be noticeable. If the train's velocity is not a significant portion of the speed of sound, you will not notice the effect. The same is true of distant galaxies; their velocity has to be a significant portion of the speed of light for the redshift to be noticed. Light is shifted toward the red because red is the lowest wavelength of visible light, corresponding to lower pitched sound. (There are portions of some nearby galaxies that are actually swinging toward us. Their light is *blueshifted*, or moved toward the upper, "higher pitched" end of the spectrum.)

The extreme redshifting of extremely distant galaxies poses some metaphysical problems. The light from these objects is so distorted that it is only with difficulty that we can call it an "object" at all. What about light that is so attenuated that its wavelength has dropped down into the infrared or radio wave range? Is it still an object? Is there some material thing "out there" that this light, or used-to-be light, "represents"? If so, where and when is the "real" object? What we are looking at is light from something that is billions of light-years away and billions of years old. Where is it now?

The difference between what is actually seen (the light) and what is supposed to be there independent of perception (the material object) is so great at dimensional extremes that one is forced to question the meaning of the latter. Descartes would say that the light is a secondary quality of perception and that the primary qualities (the real ones) apply only to the material object itself. But Descartes did not know about what happens at the edge of the universe. His mythology matched the world that he lived in; but his world is to ours what a medieval villager's would be to his.

As we look out into space, we are also looking back into time. As you look at a star 100 light-years away, you are really looking at it as it was 100 years ago. It has taken the light 100 years to get to you, and you have no way of knowing what the "real" star is doing now, if "now" has any meaning at all in this context. But the fact that we can look back in time as we look out in space has wonderful implications for cosmological research: we can look to the outer edge of space and see things happening near the beginning of time! The only thing that keeps us from seeing *everything that has ever happened* is the blockage of intervening objects. We can see as far back in time as we can see out in space. If we are able to see past our own atmosphere and around stars and gas in our own galaxy, and past other galaxies and quasars, we will be able to see genesis itself. And we will.

But it will not be a clear image. No matter how powerful our telescopes, they will not be able to resolve images in extremely deep space. There is a limitation built into the structure of the space–time that will keep us from knowing exactly where objects begin and where they end. Space, of course, has no outer edge. It just keeps getting more and more stretched out the farther you look, and the objects in it become less and less distinct. Or it might be better to say that the wavelength of light coming from extremely distant space becomes so long that it is less and less resolvable into distinct objects. If you look out far enough, everything seems to blend into an amorphous soup of background radiation without any distinct source. There are no objects distinct from other objects. This is the original "fireball," or "cosmic egg," from which our universe has evolved. We still "see" it in the form of the cosmic background radiation.

But why do we see it in all directions? The fireball originated at a single point, or "singularity," and had evolved to only a tiny fraction of the universe's size today when it began emitting the radiation we now detect. If the universe is so much larger now, and still expanding, how can the original fireball be all around us?

According to Einstein's General Theory of Relativity, mass curves space–time. The more massive a body is, the more curvature there is. The original fireball contained all the mass in the universe and curved space–time so drastically as to bring it back into itself. As we look out in different directions into space now, the lines we are looking along actually converge in deep space. Nearby, the lines radiate apart from each other, but in the extreme distance, which is also the extreme past, they begin to come together again. This is due to the extreme concentration of mass at that time. This is why the cosmic background radiation comes from all directions. We are still "in" the same space–time, still in the fireball that is no more.

We will never be able to see past (before) the fireball because gravity (the space–time curvature) was so intense then that no radiation was able to escape. But if we *could* see past it, all of space would converge on a single point, the singularity from which the fireball originated. If the universe began as a single point of space–time, which most cosmologists agree it did, that point is still around us, in all directions.

"Black holes" also contain singularities, or points of extremely curved space–time. They are like local edges of the universe in that space–time is so concentrated by gravity that light cannot escape. They are formed by extreme concentrations of mass, usually collapsed stars or whole galaxies, where gravity is so strong that atomic structure collapses. Forces are so strong that there are no recognizable objects in black holes, no electrons orbiting nuclei, no differentiation of any kind, and certainly nothing that we would recognize as matter. And if there were, we would never see it. The gravitational intensity is so great in the vicinity of a black hole that light trying to escape is pulled back. It is impossible to see past the "event horizon," or vicinity near the black hole where light is sucked in. This makes for some interesting physical phenomena.

Let us say that you and I are traveling through space one day near a black hole and you decide to jump in. You would feel the exhilaration of the fall, but you would not notice any slowing of time. You bring your space–time box with you as you fall down toward and through the event horizon and into the black hole. You still do not notice any differences in the passage of time as you look at your watch. But you may notice, as you get closer, that gravitational forces are pulling your molecules apart. You may notice some discomfort as what is left of your body collides with the undifferentiated mass at the center of the hole. But you would notice nothing else out of the ordinary. You should know, however, before you try this, that it is physically impossible for you, or anything else, to come back out once you cross the event horizon. If light is not fast enough to get out, neither are you. You will be gone forever.

But from the spaceship outside the event horizon I will never be able to see you go in. From within my space–time box you appear to slow down as you get closer and closer to the event horizon, to the point where you never actually get there. I will never see you cross over to the other side. The closer I see you get, the slower time passes; your image will just fade away. Mass slows time; extreme mass slows time to a standstill.

Quantum Mechanics

IT TAKES ENERGY TO PERCEIVE THINGS. THERE HAS TO BE LIGHT, SOUND, FORCE, or a chemical reaction impacting the body somewhere for us to be aware of physical things. The energy of perception may be very small and is not the same thing as the energy of the perceived object. It takes a fairly small amount of light energy, for instance, to see a truck roaring down the highway, while it takes a great deal of energy to move it. They are not the same.

But the energy of perception is not always small compared to that of the object perceived. If you are looking at subatomic particles instead of 18-wheelers, the energy of perception can interfere with what you are looking at. In material terms, the photon it takes to locate an electron gives the electron a little push as it "bounces off," so that you no longer know where the electron is. It is like using your fingertips to locate balloons floating through a dark room. You know where they are when you touch them, but touching them sends them somewhere else. Your energy of perception is comparable to that of what you are perceiving. That is the problem in subatomic physics: The energy needed to see what is going on messes up what is being looked at. *Seeing itself* enters into the physics of what is seen. This limits what can be known.

Werner Heisenberg (1901–1976) summed up the problems in his famous Uncertainty Principle: If you know a particle's location, you cannot know its momentum (its mass and velocity); if you know its momentum, you cannot know its location. You can know a little about both momentum and location, but not everything about both. The more you know about one, the less you can know about the other. It is a question not of the unknown, but of the unknowable. And it is not a matter of technology. No matter how big and fancy your microscopes and particle accelerators, you will never see more than reality itself allows. The world itself is different on the "quantum level": Space, time, and mass, the components used to measure location and momentum, simply do not operate at extremely small dimensions the way they do on the macroscopic level. Electrons and protons do not behave like tables and chairs.

Photons bumping off electrons and the Uncertainty Principle are descriptions of the quantum level as it looks from the point of view of the macroscopic level. But it is a mistake to try and understand this unfamiliar world in terms of the familiar; it is just too different. The mental tools we normally use to grasp things are useless in quantum physics and even detrimental. They get in the way. We have to look from where we are, it is true, but we have to try to understand what we see on its own terms. This is especially important in quantum mechanics because the quantum world is more fundamental than "our own" macroscopic world. Our world is a special structure built on top of the quantum world. Concepts that are primary to our world, such as space and matter, are not separate from one another in the quantum world. They are part of something more primary. We think of space and matter as fundamental to reality itself, but they are fundamental only to the province of reality with which we are most familiar.

Space, time, and mass, for instance, are derived from momentum, though it appears the other way around in the macroscopic world. The momentum of tables and chairs is measured by finding their mass and their velocity and then multiplying these two components by each other. Momentum equals mass times velocity. A heavy thing moving slowly may have the same momentum as a light thing moving fast. Macroscopic momentum, therefore, is a derived quantity, calculated in terms of parts that are distinct in themselves. But this is not the case on the quantum level. On the quantum level momentum cannot be divided into neat components of mass and velocity. An electron can be said to have so much momentum, but it cannot be said which part is mass and which part velocity. Momentum is a more fundamental "substance" than either. Mass and velocity are derived quantities carved out of momentum. Somewhere between the scale of electrons and tables and chairs these components arise as separate entities. But what, then, are mass and velocity? Why do they exist in their own right only on the macroscopic level?

Velocity is also a derived quantity on the macroscopic level. The velocity of tables and chairs is found by measuring how much space they traverse and how much time it takes them to do it, and then dividing the space component by the time component: meters per second or miles per hour. Mass times velocity is the same thing as mass times space divided by time. Space, time, and mass, the three components of momentum, are the three components in terms of which everything in the universe is measured: length, width, weight, force, pressure, energy, acceleration, etc. It appears as though the world itself, as we see and measure it in our everyday lives, arises from a more fundamental level of being somewhere around the scale of atomic and subatomic particles.

Our world of space and time arises from the quantum world and not the other way around because our world disappears below the quantum level, while the quantum world does not go away in ours. We do not notice quanta in our world because they are so small. But they are there. Our world only appears smooth and continuous. If you look closely enough at our world you would notice that it is chopped up into bumpy little quanta that make the picture "grainy," like a blown-up photograph. A baseball flying over center field looks like it is moving perfectly smoothly, but it is really jerking along through space, jumping from one set of tiny little lights to another, as if it were on a giant three-dimensional computer screen. The quantum world is very much there beneath everything we see and do. It is a grainy world we live in, but so finely grained that no one knew it until Max Planck saw the first grains in 1900.

Planck noticed in that year that objects could only emit or absorb radiant energy in irreducible bits, or "quanta." Einstein showed in 1905 (in the *same issue* of the physics journal that contained his Theory of Special Relativity!) that visible light is "quantized." (Photons are light "quanta.") This meant that light was not just waves, as was previously thought, but also particles, but never waves and particles at the same time. And it meant that the only way we can see things is in terms of discontinuous "dots" of energy. The world is quantized because light is quantized. Niels Bohr (1885–1962) demonstrated this in 1913 when he applied the concept of quantum mechanics to atomic structure. Electrons, he showed, could only exist at certain "energy levels" at distinct distances from the nucleus of an atom. They could not exist between energy levels because, in essence, there is no space there.

New knowledge of quantum reality has stretched the concept of material substance to a breaking point. There is a wider gulf than ever between what is actually perceived and what is supposedly "out there" making us see it. We assume when we see a series of dots representing the path of a subatomic particle that there "really is" something tying the dots together, not just our minds connecting them into a pattern. But it is meaningless to say that there is anything other than the points themselves because there is nothing, and can be nothing, in the intervals between them. We have to fill in the gaps with our minds. We cannot even say for sure that it is *the same* particle creating the dots. That they seem to be in a line does not assure us that a single particle "caused" them each to be there. The pattern merely suggests it.

The mind connects disconnected dots into patterns all the time, not just on the quantum level. A newspaper photograph is a good example. If you look closely you can see the "quanta" of which it consists. The pattern is there in little ink dots of varying sizes, but nowhere between the dots. You provide the pattern between the dots. The quantum world is like an enormous newspaper photograph with much smaller dots and more than two dimensions. The macroscopic world is the same world viewed from a distance.

But how big are the quanta? At what size does the macroscopic world merge with the quantum world? The world becomes quantized, or I should say, the space–time–mass world emerges from the quantum world, where the wavelike nature of light emerges from the particlelike nature of light. Light again! We have already seen in relativity theory that the interrelation of space, time, and mass is connected to the speed of light, and that mass and energy are related in terms of the square of the speed of light: Now we are seeing that the world is also built on its most fundamental level on the structure of light. The world, at least as we *see* it, comes to us in the form of photons.

Descartes would say that there is something behind the photons making them come to us the way they do, but Descartes did not know about quantum mechanics and relativity theory. We know that the world we *see* is structured the way light is structured. It would be simplistic to say that the world is "nothing but" light, but this does not tell us where patterns of photons come from. Could there still be material particles creating the patterns we witness? If there are, these particles are *themselves* structured the way light is. "Matter," even if there could be said to be such a thing, comes in particles or waves the same way light does. The only difference is that "matter" has mass and light does not. Mass is the additional dimension assumed by a group of photons as it becomes a pattern, or an object.

The "two slit" experiment and the phenomenon of "de Broglie waves" show this best. Light from a single source is passed through a screen with two small slits and allowed to shine on a photographic plate behind the screen. The two slits act as separate sources, so that light waves coming through one slit interfere with those coming through the other. The result is a simple "interference pattern" of alternating bright and dark bands on the photographic plate. This is a well-known phenomenon caused by wave crests and troughs from each source "adding up" to twice the intensity in the bright bands and "canceling out" at the dark bands. Only waves create this pattern, and it was this two slit apparatus and the resulting pattern that proved the wave nature of light in the nineteenth century. Water or sound waves make the same type of pattern when two wave sources interfere.

The alternating bands prove that light is a wave. But if the intensity of the light is turned way down, and one of the slits is closed, particles of light hit the photographic plate in the form of *individual* photons. Modern instrumentation is such that photons can be detected hitting the plate one at a time. As the intensity is turned down even more, there are fewer photons, not smaller ones. Light is not a steady stream of substance, but a series of discontinuous quanta in the form of photons. This proves the particle nature of light. If the light is "monochromatic" (of one color) the bundles come in only one wavelength and energy level. Because there is only one slit open there is no interference, and all the photons pile up in a single blob on the photographic plate. This shows that light is both a wave and a particle. But there is more.

If the light is turned down even more, so that only *one photon at a time* leaves the light source, each one will pass through the slit and hit the plate without the possibility of interference from other photons. Over time the photons continue to pile up in a single blob, as before. But if the other slit is opened, something interesting happens. If light truly consists of particles, each individual photon should go through one slit *or the other* and pile up in a blob behind one slit *or the other.* Two blobs should show up on the plate. But instead, the interference patterns show up again! Each individual photon, as it flies *alone* from the source to the plate, is "interfering" not with other photons, but with *itself,* as if it were itself a wave. But if it can go through only one of the slits, how does it "know" that the second slit is open? Does it somehow pass through *both* slits? What tells each individual photon that it should land in a blob when one slit is open, and in bands when two are open?

Light, therefore, is both a wave *and* a particle, but never both at the same time. The answer it gives depends on the question asked. When it is passing through space it is a wave and when it hits something it is a particle. On the macroscopic level it is mostly wavelike, and on the quantum level mostly particlelike. But our attempts to describe light are based on macroscopic concepts that simply do not work in the level of reality in which we are dealing. Light is something more fundamental than either waves or particles. It depends on how we *perceive* light — whether we are *seeing* it or *feeling* it. But more of that later.

Louis de Broglie (1892–1987), a younger contemporary of Einstein, was intrigued by the two-slit experiment and carried its implications even farther. He reasoned that if light, which everyone had thought was a wave, could act like a particle at times, maybe particles could be made to act like waves at times. Rather than hard little balls of matter, subatomic particles might be somewhat "spread out" in space with no discrete surface boundaries. De Broglie was guessing, but his ideas were later proven experimentally. The same two-slit apparatus was used, but instead of a beam of light, a beam of electrons was used. As before, the intensity of the beam was turned way down to where there was only one particle at a time passing from the source to the plate. The particles were not, therefore, interfering with each other. With one slit open, a single blob appeared on the photographic plate behind the slit, as was the case with light. But with both slits open the bands showed up! Each particle was showing a wavelike nature and interfering with itself just like light! "de Broglie waves" show that "matter" has the same basic structure as light.

Light waves and de Broglie waves are of the same fundamental nature; the difference between them is that de Broglie waves are smaller and more difficult to detect. The greater the mass of the object, the smaller its waves. The baseball flying over center field would be massive enough to have such tiny waves as to be hardly worth mentioning, but small or not, the waves are there. That is what makes it jerk from one set of quanta to another. The ball is a particular pattern that the light waves have taken; the mass of the ball maintains its identity as it moves through space and interacts with other patterns.

Because light has no mass, its waves are relatively large. But there is no *essential* difference between light waves and de Broglie waves. Mass is a structural difference in the pattern that light waves take; it is not an essential difference in the waves themselves.

WE FIND AT EXTREMES OF VELOCITY, DISTANCE, MASS, AND SIZE THAT THE DIMENsional universe breaks down as an absolute structure of physical reality. Things that look normal in the middle latitudes of everyday life become distorted farther away from home, and the distortions get worse the farther away we get. The dimensional world is a context for what we perceive in everyday life — a framework for the macroscopic level of reality — but it is specific to that reality. It is not reality itself. It is a special structure built on top of the quantum world. We have come to understand this only recently because human experience was limited to macroscopic dimensions before the turn of the twentieth century.

We find at dimensional extremes that the structure of the universe is the same as the structure of light. Light is more fundamental than space and time. Things cannot go faster than or be smaller than light because that is what they are made of. There is no medium for light in the physical world because light is not in the physical world. The physical world is in light.

Light is visual consciousness itself.

Chapter 6

The Dimensional Structure of Consciousness

ORDERLY AND MEANINGFUL EXISTENCE IS IMPOSSIBLE WITHOUT MYTH. MYTH organizes life into recognizable patterns and creates within itself a structural basis for belief and action, the means by which we stay sane and alive. Myth is understanding; it connects doing with being in everyday life.

If a myth begins to fail, a new myth will rise in its place. But the new myth must be better than the old one. If there is a failure now of current mythology, it will be because a new myth explains what we know and who we are, and gives us a better idea of what to do. It will explain both modern science and everyday experience, and give us a better sense of what human life means at this point in evolution. It will speak to the human condition. It will live and breathe within and around the society it creates, serving to comfort, to agitate, and to inspire. It will help us understand our capacity to destroy the living world, and to destroy ourselves deliberately. It will relate humanity to the physical world, but also to the biological world and to itself. In the process of redefining what the world is, it will redefine who we are. We will invent it, and it will reinvent us.

The new myth will be far more than science and far more than anything we can say here. But it will begin with science, and physics in particular, because physics is the connection between the mental and the material, the interface between self and world, and thus the link between two realms that are no longer separate. The great change will happen here. A new mythology of life will begin with physics because physics is the study of what is. Physics is our approach to creation. No one will be more surprised than the physicists.

A new myth will have to assume as little as possible. Assumptions cannot be avoided altogether, as all myths are built on assumptions, but the fewer they are and the more deeply embedded in the unknowable, the more powerful and enduring will be the world they uphold. A new myth must also be true. It will be true because truth will be built into the myth itself. Myths are always true because they define what truth is. This does not mean that truth can be anything, only that it exists within a context based on mythical assumptions. Myths are true from within and false from without. There is no way to compare the truth of one myth to that of another. One myth cannot replace another by logical process, only through incremental leaps of faith: One set of beliefs grows in time to look better than another. There is a gradual shift in the standpoint from which one understands knowledge. As the shift occurs, there are changes in understanding and in the understander. A new myth creates a new world and a new society within the world.

How will we know when myth fails and that new myth has arisen? Myth creates understanding from that which cannot be understood; without it there is only chaos. We will know that a myth has failed when we peer into the chaos and see nothing. When there is experience without understanding, and without any way to understand, we will have seen the horror of the uncreated. When we look in some unusual direction or at some extremity and find no world there, we will have seen through reality to being itself. New experience will be pushing at the gates and will one day overwhelm the world we have created within the gates.

A new myth will reach beyond the frontiers of the old, venturing past the outer defenses of current thinking, and penetrate farther into the unknowable than we have ever gone before. Uncertainty, paradox, and enigma will be its raw material. What is found in the unknowable will be the basis of a new order of things that will be meaningful for a new direction in human life. It will rise from the chaos, but will not be chaotic; it will be not life itself, but a means of living. The old myth will be exposed as untrue, and the new myth clothed in its own untruth.

The revolution will begin with the unknowable. To witness it, look at the assumptions underlying the current worldview and watch how they withstand the onslaught of new knowledge. The things that we were forced to admit are where the attack will come. The truths that *had to be* to sustain reasonable living will be shown to be untrue. The foundations of our psychic structure will be shaken, and perhaps destroyed. Much of the superstructure will remain, but the foundation will go.

A new myth will create a world within which relativity theory and quantum mechanics can operate comfortably. But it must also be a world in which we may live comfortably ourselves; if the new myth rejects the concept of matter, as I believe it will, it will have to explain why we seem to experience matter in everyday life. Most likely, what we now call physical reality will be shown to be a special case of a much broader reality.

A new myth will likely say that "reality" is experience in *any* form, not just dimensional, or "objective," experience. Ideas, thoughts, spirits, dreams, feelings, and hallucinations actually experienced will be as real as tables and chairs, only outside of space or time. Images are either in or out of dimensions. An image in time but not space is a thought; an image in time *and* space is a perception. An image in neither is just an image. This redefinition of reality will accompany a shift of assumptions from "consciousness in space–time" to "space–time in consciousness," and does not constitute a separate assumption. It merely puts nondimensional experience on an equal semantic footing with dimensional experience. "Objective" and "subjective" are not separate and not unequal, but structurally related elements of the same reality, and composed of the same primal substance.

When reality is limited to the material world, thought, emotion, imagination, spirit, and life itself are reduced to complex neural–mechanical processes, or they are avoided entirely. They are understood as observed from the outside, which is to say that they are understood not at all. Subjective experience makes no appearance in the form of material substance. It is beyond the reach of what can be verified in material terms and beyond the bounds of scientific study. There are scientists who deny that it even exists. Others admit its existence because it is absurd to deny it, but have no idea what to do with it. Most ignore it altogether. It simply does not fit into the world of matter. Even the mention of subjective phenomena in scientific circles produces apologies and embarrassment. As I write this I am aware that the word *spirit* will provoke in some readers a fear that I am going to get religious.

I promise I will not — at least, any more than I have gotten already. I will not bend scientific knowledge into categories that were there before the knowledge was there, to the extent that I am aware. I will not fit God into ideas or pronouns. And I will not ask God to clean up epistemological scraps I leave behind. The ideas I express work with or without an idea of God. To say that God is beyond ideas, that He or She is pure being, and everything, and nothing in particular, sounds trite, but it is what I mean. God is not an opinion or a theory. Belief in God is a myth and I partake of it knowingly. It is a naïveté that makes life meaningful.

By extending "reality" to conceptual consciousness, we have not placed it within the bounds of scientific analysis, only on an equal status with experience that is within the bounds of science. Consciousness in the sensory realms is "objective" in the sense that other observers can verify it. We all report that we see, hear, and smell more or less the same things, only from different perspectives in space and time, and these differences can be factored out. That makes sensory experience analyzable by the scientific method. Experience that is conceptual and not sensory is not verifiable by others and cannot be analyzed scientifically. Conceptual experience does not take place in space, while sensory experience does. The difference between conceptual and sensory experience is not, then, "reality," but dimensional structure — the only difference.

This might sound like an assumption to some. I do not argue that it is not. But I call it a "redefinition." I am including conceptual experience in my definition of reality only so that you will pay more attention to it. Whether it is really real or not does not matter, so long as you look at it as valid. Thought and imagination are valid. They are "real." They are fuzzier than physical objects, but real nonetheless. If you imagine a piece of pie you cannot taste it and touch it, and no one else can verify that you imagined it, but you did imagine it, and that is a real experience. It has no mass and it is not in space, but your experience of it is valid. The image exists even though it may not be as clear as a visual image in space. It is the image, no matter how "imaginary," that makes it possible to *do* something with a physical object. If you see a physical piece of pie in space and time, you cannot pick it up and taste it without thinking a nonphysical image of doing so. I am redefining that thought-image as "real," even though it is not within space or mass.

This is how I will get around the "assumption" that conceptual consciousness is as real as sensory consciousness. It is a word game, I realize. I will get around my assumption that matter does not exist with another linguistic sleight of hand. I will call it a *nonassumption* that it *does* exist — another word game. There is no logic to it. You just have to see if it works.

Descartes and Berkeley also played with the definition of reality. Descartes claimed that only the "primary" qualities of perception (mass, extension, number, motion, etc.) were real, while the "secondary" qualities (color, taste, smell, etc.) were unreal because they existed only in the mind of the perceiver. His emphasis was on the universe of matter in motion, or on what could be verified by any observer at any time. It was his purpose at that time to move human thought away from opinion and superstition. Subjective experiences, such as different colors perceived from the same object under different lighting conditions, could be deceiving, and had to be eliminated from the realm of the ultimately real. Berkeley claimed that *both* primary and secondary qualities were in the mind and *both* real. For him there was no reality outside the mind, and no such thing as the material substance that Descartes needed to account for the special status of the primary qualities of perception. Berkeley's emphasis was directly on being, on the immediate spiritual experience of perceptual reality. God does not need a material medium through which to show us that we are alive. The difference between physical reality and subjective experience is simply the difference between God's experience and our own. Physical reality is the mind of God; we share His experience directly to the extent that we come to know the physical world directly. Verification among multiple observers is our common experience of God.

Berkeley would say that perceptual experience, primary or secondary, is real because it is the mind of God Himself. *Conceptual* experience, on the other hand, is our own mind and tends to stray from the mind of God. This is why perceptual images are more distinct, durable, and orderly than conceptual images, and more real. I go further than Berkeley on conceptual consciousness. I admit the greater clarity, generally, of perceptual images, but say that the reason for it is that they are experienced within dimensions: It is their context, and not their content, that makes them more distinct, orderly, and durable than conceptual images. They are equally real. My emphasis is, therefore, on the primal equivalence of all experience: perceptual, conceptual, or otherwise. There are distinct structural differences among these, but they are equally valid. For this discussion I will call primary perception "observational consciousness" (in that it is available to all observers), secondary perception simply "perceptual" or "sensory," and ideation and imagination, etc., "conceptual" consciousness. I have assumed nothing by creating these definitions, and I certainly have changed nothing about the world by creating them. They are no better than anybody else's definitions, certainly no more real, and their only purpose is to shift the focus of attention from the commonplace view of reality toward what I hope is a better view. I recognize the mental effort required on the reader's part to grasp and hold on to somebody else's definitions, and I hope that they serve more than my own convenience.

This is a holistic view of life experience: We need posit the existence of nothing but being itself. We have to believe that much, but do not have to invent anything that we do not actually experience. Also, there is no causal relation between physical objects in the world and the act of observation: They are one and the same. There are no physical objects that are not observed. There is no seer and no seen, only the seeing. We need not discover the means by which physical reality becomes conscious experience because it is never anything else. Consciousness does not fit into the world of physics; physics fits into the world of consciousness.

We have to connect physics and consciousness at this point in human history because our new physical knowledge involves the act of observation — something we did not know before and still do not understand. Where it was previously thought that an event in the physical world could take place without conscious observation, it is now clear that it cannot; what we will suggest here is that a physical event can be understood *only* as an act of observation.

Consequently, we do not have to ask how consciousness "affects" material objects.

This vastly simplifies the worldview within which physics must operate. It does not, however, explain the *apparent* existence of material substance. Nor does it explain the apparent existence of other consciousnesses. Common sense still tells me that there has to be something out there causing me to touch the same thing that I see, and also causing you to see it. There has to be a reason why separate realms of perceptual consciousness agree, and separate observers agree on what they are experiencing. The evidence for matter is strong despite the evidence against it. But the agreement among perceptual realms can be shown to be the result of a correspondence between each realm and a dimension. The agreement among observers can *also* be shown to be a result of the *same* dimensional structure of consciousness. That this structure of consciousness exists is, I admit, an assumption. But it explains both the agreement among the five senses *and* the agreement among multiple observers. The fact that both are explained by the *same assumption* indicates that it is a good one.

The remainder of this chapter is treacherous reading. It is not for the faint of heart, and some readers may find it impassable. But I do not want to leave anything out. It includes details and sidelines that, while hopefully answering questions the most critical reader might pose, may distract and confuse the more general reader. You are welcome to as much of it as you please. If you find the overall idea attractive, perhaps you will come back to this section later.

Readers may also notice that I use what appear to be material terms to describe immaterial phenomena. I speak of air molecules bouncing off eardrums, photons arriving from distant galaxies, and chemicals passing through cell membranes. This is indirect, nonperceptual experience; we do not actually hear individual air molecules, and what we know of cell membranes and distant galaxies comes from what other people tell us about what they see, or see evidence of, through microscopes and telescopes. But I do not mean to imply existence of any of these phenomena outside of conscious experience. They do not, therefore, constitute material reality of any sort. They are mental abstractions that we experience symbolically in a space–time context on what I will later call the "image screen."

The "Box" versus the "Screen"

THE UNIVERSE IS A BIG BOX THAT WE ARE IN. THE BODY IS A CAGE THAT CONsciousness is in. In the box are material objects bouncing off us and off each other, obeying the physical laws to which they are subject. Some, as we, are "conscious," and behave differently. We call them "animals." If they talk, we call them "people." If we are physicists, we call them "observers." Consciousness is inside their bodies the way it is inside our own. The box is more fundamental than anything else because everything else is in it. There are four unknowables: space and time (the box itself), matter, and consciousness. Einstein, in his Special Theory of Relativity, was able to reduce this to three by combining space and time into "space–time." We know how space–time works but we do not know what it is. We have to accept that it just *is*, because we have to start somewhere. It works, and that is good enough to get us through the day.

The "box" works because it explains everything that we experience. I bump into things in space because they are there waiting for me to bump into them. If they are not in motion, I will bump into them again tomorrow in the same place. They are there with me, in space and time, and that is why I see them whenever I happen to look their way. You see them too, because like me, you have consciousness. Nobody knows what consciousness is, but it seems to be some strange plasmic substance flowing through, or with, the electrons in our brains. These electrons create, or are, mental images that reflect the material reality of our surroundings. Light and sound waves bounce off material objects and are converted into electrons as they enter our eyes and ears. The brain somehow turns these impulses into consciousness — that is, into being. Images in the brain are imperfect re-creations of real objects in the real world outside the brain.

THE BOX MYTH HAS WORKED SO WELL FOR SO LONG THAT IT IS A SHAME TO disturb it now. Even with physical evidence mounting against it, it looks good in everyday life. But in everyday life we do not see over the horizon. In everyday life the earth looks flat.

I want to replace the "box" with what I call the "screen" in order to get doing inside of being. Space and time are not as fundamental as we have thought, matter does not exist, and consciousness is everything. Perceptual consciousness is a sort of multidimensional screen on which objects of perception are located. We cannot locate consciousness itself in the brain, or in electrons, or anywhere else on the screen because everything, including the screen, is in *it*. Consciousness is the only unknowable and I will call it "being" and leave it at that, hoping you know what I mean. Space and time are *structures* of consciousness that coordinate and organize what we see and hear and touch on the screen. Empty space–time is a blank screen. When there is no actual perception, potential perception is empty space–time. What appears to be matter is the coordination of separate realms of consciousness into dimensions: Each dimension *corresponds* to a perceptual realm such as seeing or touching. I touch an object where I see it because the tactile and visual realms of consciousness are coordinated at that point in space and time. Light and sound do not bounce off material objects in space–time; they *are* the visual and auditory realms of perception. They are the actual experience of perceiving objects on the screen. Light is visual consciousness. Sound is auditory consciousness.

But light is more than this in that the space–time structure of the entire screen is derived from the space–time structure of light, and not from sound or any other perceptual realm. All the other realms are experienced in space and time dimensions based on the structure of light. Touch, taste, smell, and hearing are experienced when and where they *would be seen.* The mind has taken the dimensional order in which we see things and used it as a format within which to experience the nonvisual realms, in order that a single five-dimensional world is experienced instead of five separate one-dimensional worlds. Sound could have been used for this purpose instead of light, but there are good reasons why light works better. Light is so nearly perfect a basis for the whole of perception that it was not until the twentieth century that its imperfections were noticed.

It is difficult to envision the physical universe this way because we are used to thinking of everything real being in the box, and therefore having a place somewhere. When we look at the box itself, it is difficult to find a place to put it. We naturally look for a context within which to understand what we are considering. If you try to envision visual consciousness as a four-dimensional screen, you may wonder what the screen is in. But the screen itself provides the concept of "in-ness," and cannot be a context for itself. The only context for the screen is the whole of consciousness.

This may be difficult to envision, especially for Westerners. There is nothing specifically Buddhist or Hindu about the idea presented here, but it may be easier for some within these traditions to understand it because the box is not so deeply ingrained in their thinking. Familiarity with nonmaterial, or nondimensional, conscious experience, such as one gains in meditational practice, prepares one to accept the whole of consciousness as context for the space–time universe. This does not mean that there is any inherent conflict between Western and Eastern thought, or that one is right and the other wrong, only that the approach generally taken in the East is more appropriate in this case. Modern physics is a product of Western thought but has outgrown its own metaphysical foundations. To go farther with what it is discovering about the world it must resist the temptation to cling to its own traditions. As has been the case before, the extent to which science aims at truth over tradition is the extent to which it will continue to progress.

I hope that the screen model is a better way to understand the physical phenomenon of light. Scientists have had enormous difficulties trying to understand light *in* space–time and may be relieved to look instead for space–time within light. Light, as visual consciousness, is a form of being. If we come to understand dimensions within light, and doing within dimensions, we have come to understand doing within being.

From where you are right now, look around the room and think of the objects you see as patterns of photons on something like a four-dimensional computer or television screen. The screen is space–time, and each object a range of points of light (photons) indicating where you see something, and also where you *would feel* something were you to put your finger there. Conversely, where you touch things on the screen is where you *would see* them were you to turn your head in that direction. The arm of the chair you feel under your elbow can be seen exactly where you are feeling it. Even if you never bother to look there, you know you would see the arm of the chair there because you feel it there. All you actually experience as you look and feel about the room are visual and tactile images. Their coordination in space–time gives you the impression that there is something outside of either vision or touch causing them to occur at the same time and place, but you will try for now to resist the temptation to call it matter. For now you will simply notice that your visual and tactile realms of perception are dimensionally coordinated on the screen.

It will not be too much more to ask you to think of the three remaining realms of perception in the same way. You experience auditory, olfactory, and chemical images where you *would see* them; where you do see them is where you *would hear, smell, or taste* them. The direction you hear a sound coming from is where you would turn your head to see it. Where you smell or taste something is a little less defined, and there are good reasons for this, as I hope to show, but generally speaking, where you see something is where you would smell or taste it if you wished to do so. Where and when you perceive something in one realm does not tell you *how* you will experience it in any other realm, only where and when. Seeing a ham sandwich on the table in the kitchen does not tell you anything about how it will taste, only where you will have to go to taste it. An object's location in any one sensory realm is a "hyperlink" to the same location in any other realm. The shape of the object you see in space does not tell you how it will be heard or smelled, only where. The object's shape is a range of points in space, each one of which indicates potential perception. A train could have a bell on one end and a whistle on the other end; you might see one long range of visual points, but hear two distinct auditory images.

Now, I will ask you to do one more thing. You may have come along for the ride so far, but what I will ask you next may prove too much for you. I must ask it because the dimensional structure of consciousness does not work without it. I have shown you already, I hope, that it is at least possible to understand physical reality without the help of material substance, but only from the standpoint of *your own experience*. The dimensional coordination of the perceptual realms on the screen explains why you touch something where you see it, but not why *someone else* sees it there, too. To explain this I am going to have to ask you to get rid of his consciousness, as a separate something inside his brain, and pay attention only to what you *actually* experience. You do not experience his actual consciousness in any case, or mine, for that matter. Consciousness in other people is like material substance in this respect: You have no direct experience with it, but you need it to make sense of what you experience in the "box." With the screen, we can be rid of consciousness-in-observers *the same way* we are rid of matter-in-objects. We can show that the apparent existence of consciousness in other people (or plants or animals) is due to the *same* structure of consciousness that lends apparent material substance to physical objects.

But before we go any farther, I want to emphasize that when we get rid of consciousness "in" other people, we also get rid of it "in" you. You do not have consciousness in your brain, or your electrons, or anywhere else. It is not in your self, any more than it is in myself or anybody else's self. Self is in it, and as we have already said, everything else is in it, too. This is the hard part. It is enough to ask you to understand physical reality without matter, but now I am must tell you that the "observers" you see in space and time, even your closest relatives and best friends, do not have consciousness *in* them any more than they have matter. We are used to associating consciousness with self, but we will have to rid ourselves of this habit. Consciousness is independent of self. The self exists in order to do, but not in order to be.

There are enormous ethical consequences in what I have just said. To go into them in any detail now would be a diversion from the main course of discussion, but it is important to point out now that the nonexistence of consciousness in observers does not mean that they are not alive, that they do not feel or hurt, or that they are merely mechanical processes that can be used or manipulated the way we use or manipulate inanimate objects. Observers, be they people or dogs or blue-green algae, are an order of consciousness higher than self, and it is only through transcendence of self that this it realized. Being is not in self, or in the doing that creates self. This is the ultimate importance of what I am saying in this book.

What, then, do you *actually experience* about observers that is different from inanimate objects? They move differently, for one thing. They seem to be able to navigate around other objects in space–time that "unconscious" objects would bump into. There is a certain *order* to their motion. Also, people observers, and to a lesser extent animals, are able to communicate what *they say* they are experiencing. You do not actually experience what they are perceiving; all you actually perceive are sights and sounds from their mouths or pens or word processors. But there is a particular *order* to these sights and sounds that gives them significance over and above ordinary sights and sounds. We call it language. Language has physical as well as literary properties. The order implicit in language is the same type of order you noticed in the way noncommunicating observers avoid bumping into things, only a much more highly refined form. Language is *reducible* to sights and sounds, the way a building is reducible to bricks and mortar, but it has an intangible quality that makes communicating observers seem conscious. Actual perception is limited to grunts and ink spots, but the order in which they are arranged makes you aware of an entirely new realm of consciousness that we will call the *observational realm*. Observational consciousness is an orderly construction of perceptual parts the way visual consciousness is an orderly construction of tactile parts. It is reducible to grunts and ink spots that you hear and see the way light is reducible to the photons a retinal cell touches. But in becoming a separate realm of consciousness, it becomes a wholeness over and above its parts. It becomes as real as its parts. As soon as you accept the validity of words you hear people say, observation becomes as real as perception.

The observational realm is indicated by orderly arrangements in the perceptual realms, but it is related to perception in another way as well. It is defined as "potential perceptual consciousness," in that information from an observer is what you *would perceive* directly were you standing where he is. If he says he sees a large green book on the left-hand side of the living room table and you do not see it there, there is no dimensional coordination and no observational realm. This realm is coordinated with the perceptual realms of consciousness *in the same way* that they are coordinated with each other. That is what is so fascinating about dimensional correspondence.

Getting consciousness out of self and out of observers will be a long, roundabout process. I will introduce new terms and concepts now so that you may be familiar with them when they come up later. I give them new names only to make you see them in a new way. The picture they present will be more complicated before it becomes simpler, but will make sense in the end. The screen, I hope to show, is simpler than the box, and takes a much broader reality into account.

Dimensional Correspondence

THE PERCEPTUAL REALMS OF CONSCIOUSNESS EACH CORRESPOND TO A SPACE OR time dimension. There are five perceptual realms and five physical dimensions, including mass (which appears "foreshortened" in space–time as a second time dimension). In addition to these five there is a less defined, nonquantitative "dimension" corresponding to the observational realm of consciousness that is also foreshortened in space–time (in the form of nonuniform acceleration), as *order*. Only observers (living beings) are capable of orderly motion.

Dimensional correspondence is a guess that explains experience on both the macroscopic and quantum levels of physical reality. It is an unknowable that replaces the three unknowables (space–time, matter, and consciousness-in-observers) upholding the myth of the box.

Dimensional Interchange

AN OBSERVER EXPERIENCES APPARENT MOTION *IN* SPACE–TIME WITH AN "INTER-change" of space, time, and mass dimensions. As you interchange one space for one time dimension, all objects in the universe move at a constant velocity past you, and you have the sensation of apparent motion through space in the opposite direction. This can be thought of as "rotating" an axis of space into the time dimension. Dimensional interchange makes perceptual conscious-ness seem to move through space. A simpler space-for-space interchange would appear as a turning of your eyes in a new direction.

A more complicated interchange involves the rotation of space–time into the mass dimension. This is apparent acceleration in space. Where constant velocity involves one time dimension, (linear) acceleration involves two, and is expressed in terms of meters per second *per second*. This second time dimen-sion is the mass dimension, and corresponds to the tactile realm of percep-tion. You experience the entire tactile realm when you (apparently) accelerate. This is the "g force" that you feel every time you step on the gas, go over a bump, or happen to find yourself in a gravitational field. [3]

Dimensional interchange, particularly involving the mass dimension, appears complicated, but is really quite simple. You experience it every time you walk down the hall, turn your head, or pick up a pencil. Anything you *feel* is an acceleration and an interchange of corresponding dimensions. It may involve your entire body, or only part of it. (More often than not, what you feel in one part of your body is balanced by what you feel in another part, and there is no apparent overall acceleration.) Dimensional interchange is an important concept for understanding "doing," as all doing requires it.

You can think or dream or meditate without your body, but you cannot do anything without it.

Potential

A "POTENTIAL" IS A CONTEXT FOR INFORMATION. IT IS WHAT GIVES MEANING TO actual experience. If I say "six," it will have no meaning unless there is a context, such as "the number of runs the Cleveland Indians score in the ninth inning." The potential is the game itself in that anything *could* happen. The Indians could score no runs, or four runs, or forty-seven runs: The potential is what makes the actual events meaningful and exciting. We create the potential by building the stadium, selling the tickets, and paying people to throw balls and swing bats at them. What happens is *information* because there is a meaningful context within which to experience events. Without context "six" means nothing.

Information requires a potential in which anything, besides what does happen, could happen. The Dow Jones Industrials Average is a potential because it could go up or down, and that is why you pay attention to it. The page you are looking at is a potential in that the words and letters that actually appear on it could say anything else. That is how what I have to say gets to you. A telephone is a potential because the sounds coming out of it could be any other sounds; the particular sounds that *do* come out are intelligent because they are potentially chaotic. Potentials are what make actual experience seem "real."

A dimension is a potential in that it provides a context for actual perceptual information, and gives that experience its meaning. Photons or air molecules perceived randomly without such a context would have no significance and would not constitute physical objects. They mean physical objects only because they are in dimensions. The five potentials corresponding to the five perceptual realms are intercoordinated into what we experience as space–time–mass (the screen): What we actually experience through the senses is interesting and meaningful because it could be anything else. There exists the possibility for sensory perception at any point in any dimension.

Potentials bring complexity and meaning to experience, but they also bring a sense of nonbeing. If you hear something happen in the next room you have a sense of not seeing it, or if you smell something in the kitchen you may have a sense of not tasting it. You feel that something is going on in the world that you do not experience. The sense of nonbeing is much more severe in the case of the observational realm, which we defined as potential perceptual consciousness. You hear from other people about things happening all over town and around the world that you do not perceive directly, and feel that you are experiencing only a small part of what is "actually" happening. You may feel you are a very small bit of consciousness in a very big box. But if you go back to the screen model, you will notice that your *actual* experience of what is happening on the other side of town (what appears on the screen) is limited to the language you hear from your friends or see in the paper. What *they* say they experience is potential only. The actual universe is limited to what is experienced directly.

This is not to say that potential perception is not real. It is, in fact, a large and growing portion of the whole of consciousness. Much, if not most, of what we know of the world we learn through other people. Our direct "actual" experience is limited to the sound of words and the shape of letters on a page. Observational consciousness is a rapidly evolving structure of human consciousness to which you have access, but which you must share with all other observers. Unlike actual perception, it is the same for everyone. Scientific procedure systematically creates observational consciousness through its insistence on the verification of experimental results by any observer at anytime.

Potentials are also essential to doing. In order to do, there must be choices, any one of which *could be*. I could turn left as I walk out the front gate, or turn right; both possibilities exist until one or the other is done. "Doing" is the rotation of space–time–mass axes into the universe to the left of the front gate or into the universe to the right. But by doing, the wholeness of being is torn. If we turn left we have the sense of missing what is happening in an entire universe to the right. The existence of potentials creates worry about what could have been, and destroys the complete union of self and what is.

Tactile Reduction

EVERY PHOTON HAS A WAVELENGTH OR COLOR. IT ALSO HAS MOMENTUM. IT IS experienced as a tiny point of light in the visual realm and as a minute "touch" in the tactile realm. This means that visual experience is *reducible* to tactile experience: Seeing is "no more than" touch.

This, of course, is a gross exaggeration. It is like saying that a Gothic cathedral is "no more than" the stones of which it is made. The significance of light, and of the cathedral, is the particular order of its constituent parts. Tactile reduction is essential, however, to understanding the structural relation between the visual and tactile realms and their corresponding dimensions. The "dual nature" of light, the "graininess" of space–time, and the mass-energy equivalence are all due to tactile reduction.

The Photon Screen

THE PHOTON SCREEN IS VISUAL CONSCIOUSNESS. IT IS LIGHT ITSELF. IT CONSISTS of light quanta (photons) arranged in dimensional patterns. It is that portion of the quantum screen actualized in the form of vision.

A visual object is a pattern of photons.

The Quantum Screen

THE QUANTUM SCREEN IS PERCEPTUAL CONSCIOUSNESS AS A WHOLE. IT INCLUDES the photon screen, but is not limited to it, extending beyond it in every direction. It is hearing, smelling, tasting, and touching, as well as seeing. It is a space–time extrapolation of the structure of light, consisting of innumerable quanta, or photon-sized "bits" of energy. It does not include the observational realm. Observers appear on the quantum screen as objects capable of creating *order*, but the order they create appears on the quantum screen only in reduced, perceptual form.

A physical object is a pattern of quanta. The quantum screen is the physical world perceived directly.

The Image Screen

THE IMAGE SCREEN IS THE CONTEXT OF OBSERVATIONAL CONSCIOUSNESS. IT IS NOT direct perceptual experience, but what is experienced through other observers, in the form of symbols, such as words and numbers. It is what other observers say they perceive. It is the world created by talking to people, reading books, watching television, and listening to what astronomers tell us about the far side of the galaxy. It is potential perceptual consciousness as a whole (what anyone can see at anytime), and therefore the physical universe known through scientific investigation. Where the photon screen is vision, and the quantum screen perception as a whole, the image screen is the world beyond direct experience. All three are structurally identical, based on the equality of one second of time and c meters of space. The image screen is not, however, as clear and highly defined as the quantum screen.

The image screen is also the context of what I have called "doable thought." Images become dimensionalized on the screen before they can be done. Once done, they become observational consciousness. The fact that doable thought remains within the same context as observational consciousness indicates that, though the observational realm is growing rapidly, it is still in an early stage of development.

THE PHOTON, QUANTUM, AND IMAGE SCREENS ARE SEPARATE FACETS OF A SINGLE dimensional structure of consciousness. What is seen on the photon screen may be touched and heard on the quantum screen, and read about on the image screen. Each is linked to the other two through potential experience. Since they are separate avenues to a single entity, I refer to them collectively as the "screen."

The Observational
Realm of Consciousness

OBSERVATIONAL CONSCIOUSNESS IS DEFINED AS "POTENTIAL PERCEPTION." EVERYthing I see, you could see from where I am standing, and vice versa. What we call the "physical universe" is the observational realm in that it is what can be observed by anyone at anytime. The progress of science is the continuing evolution of the observational realm. It is experienced through symbols on the quantum screen that appear as dimensional images on the image screen.

The observational realm is structured from the perceptual realms the same way that the visual realm is structured from the tactile realm. Communication is reducible to perception the way light is reducible to touch. Turning this around, we could say that observational consciousness is a multiobserver experience built from the perceptual experience of individual people the same way that light is a multicellular experience built from the tactile experience of individual cells. The wholeness of each is built from, but not limited to, its constituent parts.

THE SCREEN, AS A MODEL FOR THE DIMENSIONAL STRUCTURE OF CONSCIOUSNESS, is better than the box, but it does not cover all of consciousness. There are some very real things, such as thought, imagination, and dreams that are not on the screen. Science restricts itself to the screen, but science can no longer claim to cover all of reality. Science looks only at the dimensionally structured part of consciousness.

For this reason the dimensional structure of consciousness is not a scientific theory. It cannot be tested within the bounds of science as currently defined because its scope is larger than science. That is why it is a myth.

The Tactile Realm of Perception

WHAT DO WE ACTUALLY EXPERIENCE? IF THE DIMENSIONAL STRUCTURE OF CONsciousness is better than the material world, why is it not readily apparent? If it is so fundamental to how we see and understand the world, why are we unaware of it?

We are unaware of it, I believe, because it is so close to us. We are like fish in water: We cannot know that it exists while we are in it. We have to jump out of the dimensions, if only briefly, to see what they are. We did this on several occasions in the twentieth century. At dimensional extremes we caught glimpses of things outside the familiar world; we saw that the dimensions are not absolute, that they do not go on forever, and that they do not contain all that is real. We went beyond what was knowable. But it is uncomfortable there, traveling near the speed of light, bouncing off photons and electrons, and falling into black holes. It is hard to breathe, and we do not want to stay there for long. We are like fish out of water. But having fallen back into the familiar, we can now see it for the first time.

It is less a matter of seeing something new than of knowing for the first time that it has been there all along. The dimensional structure of consciousness is experienced every time we reach out and touch something that we see. We know where and when to touch it because of where and when we see it: This is the dimensional structure of consciousness. It is so commonplace that we miss it. To know that it is there we have to experience the familiar all over again.

To experience the interrelation among the five sensory realms, try and do without it. Try to experience each realm in the absence of the others, pulling it apart from the other four. Spend a few minutes just hearing, or just smelling, or just seeing. This is difficult because you are used to experiencing all of the realms together, and interpret experience in any one realm in terms of experience in the others. How something tastes, for instance, has a lot to do with how it smells, and what it looks like. It is particularly difficult to experience touch separately. How you experience touch has to do with how you "envision" what is touched. The tactile realm is experienced in terms of how it *would be seen* rather than on its own terms. If you could not see anything, had never seen anything, never heard, smelled, or tasted anything, and never talked to anyone who had, you would understand the tactile realm in a very different way. Your actual experience of touch would be the same, but the context of that experience would be very different.

There would not be, for instance, a concept of space. If all experience were limited to the tactile realm, there would be no experience anywhere but on, or in, the body. Objects at a distance from the body would not be experienced at all, and would not exist at all, in a purely tactile world. There would be no such thing as an "object," only a tactile image, because without other realms of perception, there would be no way to verify the existence of an object "out there" causing tactile sensations. It takes more than one perceptual realm to create the concept of something independent of perception. You would experience the feeling itself without an overlying sense of an external object causing the feeling. Since there would be nothing beyond the body, the body would be the same thing as the world. There might be a sense of different places in or on the body, but these do not become spatial differences until the tactile realm is coordinated with vision and the other senses. If the body is everything that is actually perceived, and everything that is potentially perceived, there would be no sense of the body in space, and no sense of other bodies. If consciousness were the same thing as self, this would be a "solipsistic" existence, or one where self was all that is.

But there would be no self in a purely tactile world. Self, as a concept closely identified with the body and with a perspective in space–time, arises with the higher realms of perception and their corresponding space and time dimensions. For self to exist there must be options, choices, potentials, and the possibility of things being other than as they are. There has to be the possibility of doing. With a single realm of consciousness, tactile or otherwise, there is no potential for reality to be anything other than what it is.

The body is experienced as a single realm of consciousness in the discipline of hatha yoga. The practitioner assumes a variety of body postures, and the mind concentrates on what the body is actually feeling, directed not to the shape the body takes in space, but to kinesthetic sensations from "within." The contraction of muscles and the stretching of joints and tendons are experienced on their own terms rather than as if they were seen from the outside. There is no outside, "objective" view. Tactile images of tension, pleasure, pain, pressure, breathing, and the beating of the heart come and pass. In the absence of distracting sounds and thoughts, the body becomes the universe. Ultimately, it is an experience of pure being: Objects lose their separateness from sensation and from each other; there is no distinction between sensor and sensed, and the world and self dissolve into each other. There is movement, but no doing.

The unity of object and subject is most easily attained within the tactile realm because the tactile realm is inherently nonspatial. Seeing, hearing, and smelling, on the other hand, create the space within which they are experienced. With space there is a world separate from and beyond the body. Space means possibilities not actualized, and the existence of things not directly experienced. With space, the self comes into existence as actual experience within the context of potential experience. Doing arises with space.

But what would happen, you might ask, if a purely tactile observer were to receive a message of some sort from the "outside"? Let us say you are in your purely tactile body-equals-universe world and you feel a tap on the shoulder. If it were just a tap, it would be nothing more than a touch sensation that you would have no way of associating with an object or person. But if it were a series of taps in some sort of *order*, you would take note. You would suspect that you were not alone. A sense of order would be hard to define, and you would not be sure at first. You would wonder if the taps were really random and if you were only imagining the order. But at some point you would be sure, one way or the other. Either you would go back to the quasi-solipsism of the purely tactile world or you would be forced to admit the existence of another world that you do not experience directly. A self would arise — your self — as against whatever else it may be that created the order you have experienced. And with self arises the nonself, or the context within which the whatever else must exist. All you have actually experienced is an orderly series of tactile sensations separated in *time*, but from them a sort of space arises as a context for the perceived order. Whatever it is that creates the order is not you, and must exist beyond your purely tactile world.

This is how hearing and seeing arise from the tactile world and create the space that we are "in." Orderly series of "taps" in the form of air molecules or photons create new realms of perceptual consciousness and corresponding space dimensions. Hearing and seeing are *reducible* to touch, but they are not "nothing but" touch. They arise from tactile consciousness, but they are separate realms of consciousness existing in their own right. They are each a wholeness that is more than its parts, the way a building is more than a pile of bricks and two-by-fours. The order in which the parts exist is the manifestation of their wholeness. The building is an orderly arrangement of bricks and two-by-fours that creates a consciousness of "home," "grocery store," "civic center," etc., in the way that seeing and hearing are orderly arrangements of "taps" that create new realms of consciousness. What you are reading now is an orderly arrangement of ink on white paper, but it is more than that, I am hoping. A form of consciousness arises from the printed page the way hearing or seeing arise from tiny tactile sensations on the tympanum or the retina. They are a wholeness that is more than their constituent parts. This is why light behaves like particles when reduced to its smallest constituent parts, and why space seems to disappear below the quantum level. Space is the context within which minute tactile sensations become hearing or vision.

The body is tactile consciousness as we actually feel it and remains essentially nonspatial. This is complicated by the fact that we also *see* the body, *in space*. The body *felt* is actual tactile sensation *not in* space; the body *seen* is potential tactile perception *in* space. We do not feel space. We think of the body in space because of the dimensional coordination of tactile with visual perception; we "envision" what we feel at a location in space where we would see it. The tactile realm is not actually in space, only coordinated at the origin of space and time axes. I will try to explain what this means later in the section on light. I will partly contradict what I say here, but for now, actual tactile perception is not in space.

We tend to think of the body in space also because it appears to move in space as we "interchange" dimensions. *Doing* happens by interchanging space, time, and mass with each other. This is the same thing as rotating the axes of space–time–mass around the origin (the body.) If there is no dimensional interchange, the body is at rest. Time moves on without any change in space. But if one space dimension is interchanged for time, or the axes "tilted," the body appears to move through space at a constant velocity. The motion of all objects in the universe past the body in one direction appears as motion of the body itself in the opposite direction. Constant velocity is purely relative. Moving one object uniformly (the body) while keeping everything else stationary is the same thing, physically, as keeping the body stationary and moving the rest of the universe. We think of the body moving in space because it seems simpler than moving everything else, but it is no better from a physical standpoint. It is as good to say that the entire universe is moving the other way as we walk down the hall.

But this only works for uniform, or unaccelerated, motion. Constant velocity is relative, but acceleration is not; this is a major physical difference. It is more complicated by far to *accelerate* all the stars and planets in the universe than to accelerate one medium-sized human body. It may be as good to say that everything in the universe moves once we are *already walking* down the hall, but it is not as good to say that we can get the entire universe moving as easily as getting the body moving. The near infinite mass of all the stars and planets in the universe would take near infinite energy to accelerate. We cannot pretend, therefore, that apparent accelerated motion of the body through space is the same thing as accelerated motion of the universe in the opposite direction. But dimensional interchange is a rotation of dimensional axes, and not a rotation of the universe itself. The mass of the universe does not move — only the axes move — and the axes do not weigh anything. They are merely the context within which we perceive the stars and planets and everything else. When we begin to walk down the hall (when we appear to accelerate through space), we rotate the axes not only of space and time, but also of mass. We interchange space and time dimensions as a whole with the mass dimension as a whole, and as we rotate space and time into mass, we feel a uniform sensation throughout the entire tactile realm proportional to the magnitude of the rotation. This is the second time component of our apparent motion, the per second *per second* that distinguishes acceleration from constant velocity. There is a direct identity, then, between the "g force" of acceleration and the mass dimension. The second "per second" of our apparent motion through space is the mass dimension as a whole, and corresponds to the tactile realm of perception. It is not in space, but coordinated with space as an additional physical dimension. It appears "foreshortened" in the four dimensions of space–time the way an additional space dimension appears foreshortened on a two-dimensional surface.

Dimensional interchange, whether a simple space-for-time interchange in the case of constant velocity or a more complicated mass-for-space–time interchange in the case of acceleration, is important for the new concept I am suggesting. It should be thought of as an interrelation between the tactile and the nontactile realms of perception. Touching is related to seeing in the form of apparent acceleration of the body through space: Whenever you feel the g force, you will also see things moving by you at faster and faster velocities. This is important not only because it demonstrates that dimensions are structures within consciousness, but because it is the physics of doing. Dimensional interchange is how we do things. If we want to change what we see in the world, we rotate just the right dimensions in just the right way to get what we would like to see. If there is a chair out of order in the room, we accelerate toward it, collide with it, and knock it somewhere else, hopefully to a better, more orderly location.

In practice, we accelerate the entire body only until we touch the chair, at which point we accelerate only parts of the body (hands) to move the chair in an orderly manner. Still other parts of the body (feet) accelerate against the floor to keep the body balanced as a whole. Hands and feet move separately so that the body as a whole can remain at equilibrium. Doing can be done in this way without accelerating the body as a whole. Actual experience is always a complex of partial accelerations that tend to cancel each other out within the body and keep it more or less balanced. Apparent motion of the body as a whole through space is an overall imbalance of partial accelerations.

This description of doing as the interchange of space, time, and mass dimensions should bring up some questions. If we do not like what we see in the world, and want to rearrange it, must there be some other realm of consciousness, besides the five perceptual realms, in which we *conceive* a better arrangement? What is the connection between this realm and the perceptual realms of consciousness? Once we have made the new arrangement, what is the physical meaning of the *order* we have created? Is order quantifiable, as in space or mass? Why is it that only *living beings* are capable of creating order? Can doing only be done by beings? I will postpone answering these here. For now I will only say that doing is an interchange of space, time, and mass dimensions, the tactile realm of perception being the origin of dimensional axes. You can think anything you want, but you have to get your body behind it to get it done.

That mass can be understood as a dimension is not an especially radical idea. All measurements in the physical world are made in terms of space, time, and mass components, or meters, seconds, and kilograms. Descartes established the three space dimensions in a coordinate system that he identified with the universe itself, and Einstein established the time component as another dimension in his Special Theory of Relativity. It should not be surprising that mass would also be a dimension. That there has been no apparent physical manifestation of mass as a dimension has to do with the difficulty of seeing oneself "in" mass the way one is "in" space and time. But if space and time are structures of consciousness, as I am proposing, one is not "in" them either. The fact that mass interchanges with space and time the way space and time interchange with each other shows that it operates as a dimension in this respect. The fact that it is already on an equal status with space and time as a component of physical measurement means that physics can go on measuring things as it always has. Understanding mass as a dimension will not disturb the everyday workings of the physics profession. The physical world becomes simpler if its three components are the same thing rather than two of them world structures and the third a measure of material substance within that world.

Mass also works better as a dimension in Einstein's General Theory of Relativity. In that theory, Einstein states that space–time is "curved" in the vicinity of massive bodies like the sun. Light rays, which define lines of space, are straight lines in "empty," interstellar space, but curve slightly around the sun and around other stars. In the vicinity of extremely massive bodies such as black holes, they curve all the way back into themselves. But if space–time is four-dimensional, there has to be another dimension into which it is curved. (A two-dimensional surface such as a piece of paper can be curved by bending it over, but you need a third dimension to bend it into.) Gravity is a curvature of four-dimensional space–time into the mass dimension.

Inertia is another instance in which mass operates better as a dimension than as a measure of material substance. As mentioned before, there is no physical explanation for how mass can "cling" to space when subjected to an accelerating force. Ernst Mach (1838–1916) attempted to explain inertia as some sort of retarding force field created by all the fixed stars and galaxies in the universe instantaneously operating on all objects everywhere. It is interesting that he was trying to avoid the concept of absolute space by explaining inertia not in relation to space itself, but as a phenomenon in relation to all physical objects in space. Together all objects create a sort of "average" space against which inertia is defined. But Mach did not begin to explain how such a scheme might be possible, and he admitted that his idea was merely operational and might be replaced at anytime. If mass is a dimension, as I am suggesting, there is no need to explain inertia as an interaction between matter and space, or between one material object and the sum total of all others. An object accelerates according to its location in the mass dimension. Mass, and not matter, determines the second time component of its motion.

But how is the mass of an object related to the tactile realm of perception? We have seen in the case of the g force that the mass dimension as a whole is directly related to the tactile realm as a whole, but what about individual objects in mass? We feel the second time dimension (mass) as a whole when we are accelerated, but the second time dimension of a particular object's motion is something that we only see. We cannot measure mass by how an object feels; we can only measure mass by its behavior in space–time–time, at a distance from the body. But the measurement tells us the object's *potential* tactile perception. The more massive it is, the more we will feel it when it does touch the body. Its mass does not tell us what it will feel like, only the magnitude of tactile sensation we can expect under fixed conditions.

The tactile realm of perception is always a relation to the earth. The tactile Earth is not a shape in space but a continuous directional flow of kinesthetic sensation throughout the body. It is a permanent, uniform rotation of space–time axes into the mass dimension. It is not something we walk on but something that flows up through our feet. The earth is a heaviness and an attachment: a kinesthetic extension beyond the body. It is an equilibrium, a balance that is not always balanced, but that always returns to balance. The earth's gravity keeps us stable in the mass dimension, and its friction, an offspring of gravity, keeps us stable in the space dimensions. When we accelerate in any direction, friction made possible by the earth's gravity decelerates us in the opposite direction.

According to Einstein's Principle of Equivalence introduced in the General Theory of Relativity, gravity and acceleration are physically identical. The tactile realm has always known this. There is no tactile or kinesthetic difference between being accelerated upward and standing still on the ground in a gravitational field. Though you do not appear to be moving, the earth's ground accelerates you upward against the earth's gravity, and that is what you feel. It is the visual realm that has had trouble understanding this because it doesn't see the body accelerating in relation to objects around it. They do not accelerate because they, too, are supported by the ground. The same Earth that is the gravity is also the ground. It supports you and all objects around you against itself. The objects it does not support accelerate past you until they hit the ground. You may envision it as an enormous ball mysteriously pulling you downward as its surface keeps you up, but what you are actually feeling in your body is simply the earth.

The steadiness of the earth's tactile consciousness always returns. You may jump up into the air, increasing it momentarily, then lose it altogether as you fall back toward the ground. But it will always return when you hit the ground, exactly as it was. You may create crosscurrents by accelerating sideways down the hall or down the street, but the earth is always there beneath it all. If you escape your tactile connection with the earth for a few minutes by jumping off a tall building or out of an airplane, you will find that it accumulates in your absence. The balance returns when you return.

Even when standing still, the earth's friction keeps the tactile realm in balance. Every tactile sensation is an acceleration. Every time you touch something your entire body is pushed back the other way. Were it not for the earth, you would drift aimlessly about the universe, never returning to a familiar setting. If I were to hand you a pencil in a frictionless world, you would be unable to keep your whole body from accelerating down the hall away from me. Your velocity would stabilize as soon as I let go of the pencil, but you would keep moving until you bumped into something else, or until somebody else handed you another pencil. Then you would move aimlessly in another direction. The earth keeps your world familiar by flowing up through the back of your left leg as I hand you the pencil. The friction in the floor and the gravity keeping you against the floor restore your tactile equilibrium. One part of your body, your hand, is accelerated in one direction while another part, your leg, accelerates back, equally and opposite. There is no overall acceleration, so you stay put. The earth is your home not only because it feeds and nourishes you, but because it brings you back to what you know.

But when you jump in the car in the morning and step on the gas, the back of your seat is too much for the earth to resist. Your tactile equilibrium goes out of balance until you reach 60 miles per hour, and then out again temporarily as you go over bumps and around curves. When you stop, your equilibrium returns, but it is not the same equilibrium because of the gas pedal and all the bumps and curves you have been through. Your original equilibrium is not restored until you come back at the end of the day to where you started, having canceled out all of the morning's accelerations. That you are back where you started is something you can see, but also something you feel. You could do it without vision if you kept careful track of each of your accelerations. The earth is your home in mass as well as in space. It is part of your body.

The earth has always been there until recently. A few of us have escaped it. We have accelerated long and hard enough that the steadiness did not return. We have been where there was no friction. We now know, at the turn of the millennium, that the tactile world goes beyond the simple equilibrium of the earth. We have felt it, and will never be the same. In time we will leave home for good, but the earth will be the being from which we do it.

THE TACTILE REALM OF PERCEPTION IS THE SAME THING AS THE BODY. THE BODY *felt* is actual tactile sensation not in space, while the body *seen* is potential tactile sensation in space. When actual tactile perception is coordinated with vision (and with the other senses), the body appears to assume a location in space. But tactile experience remains fundamentally nonspatial and can be experienced as such in the absence of the other realms.

The body becomes related to space through the evolution of higher realms of consciousness. The tactile perceptions of single cells become the seeing, hearing, and smelling of multicellular organisms, and space becomes the context for that experience. Space begins as a projection of the body, but ends up a context for the body, as tactile and nontactile experiences are coordinated into a single multidimensional world.

The Chemical Realm

MORE FUNDAMENTAL EVEN THAN THE TACTILE REALM IS TASTE, OR THE CHEMICAL realm of perception. What we as multicellular organisms experience as taste began even before the enclosure of protoplasm within membranes. That taste predates touch is evidenced by the fact that cells "feel" things by sensing ionic imbalances on the cell membrane. Touch is therefore reducible to chemical stimuli. The electric field produced by the outermost electrons of an external object disturbs the polarization of potassium ions on the surface of cell membranes and causes a flow of ions toward or away from the locality of the object. The reducibility of touch to taste makes sense in that the idea of "touch" seems impossible without a cell membrane. Tactile consciousness can only have evolved in conjunction with an enclosure of some kind, separating internal from external chemistry. (Or, more accurately stated, the evolution of tactile from purely chemical perception was accompanied by what we, as multicellular organisms, understand as a spatial enclosure.) Tactile information, though it may be chemically based, is qualitatively distinct from other forms of chemical information, and constitutes an entirely separate realm of perception. The question now is: How are these two realms related to one another, and to the other realms?

Touch and taste are the only two realms of perceptual consciousness common to all living cells: plant or animal, unicellular or multicellular. All cells experience "chemotactile" perception, and only chemotactile perception. They do not see, hear, or smell. Only multicellular organisms are capable of experiencing these "higher" realms. Higher organisms evolve specialized sensory organs consisting of individual cells, each of which experiences nothing other than chemotactile sensation, but conveys higher sensory experience to the organism as a whole. The information relayed to the rest of the body is *reducible* to chemical or tactile experience, and is therefore in a form that other cells can experience. The particular *order* that the information takes, however, can only be experienced by the organism as a whole. Cells in the tympanum, for instance, experience tactile impact of air molecules that becomes "hearing" for the organism as a whole, though individually each cell "hears" nothing. Hearing becomes a medium of intercellular information, a higher dimension of multicellular life. The organism becomes a wholeness that is more than the sum of its cells.

But not all cell communities develop intercellular media and higher dimensions of multicellular life. Some never take the path toward specialized sensory organs, and remain limited to entirely chemotactile experience. We call them plants. Even such complex life forms as flowers and trees, as prolific and successful as they may be, do not see, hear, or smell. They absorb the raw energy of light but do not appreciate its information. They sense light only in its tactile form. They taste and feel, like all cellular life, but beyond this, the structure of what we may call their "perceptual consciousness" is quite limited, and entirely different from that of animals.

It does, however, exist. The chemical and tactile realms are coordinated with each other, and it is this coordination that produces a sense of "object" external to perception itself. Either the chemical or tactile realm alone, in the absence of the other, can have no subject or object of experience. A purely tactile observer, as we have already seen, cannot verify what is experienced in any other realm, and can have no idea of an external object "causing" him to feel what he feels. Either he experiences a tactile sensation or he does not. There can be no object in space separate from and beyond actual sensation, waiting to be touched. Similarly, if he can only taste, he has no way to understand his experience as a "thing" in space, beyond and outside of the chemical realm, because there is nothing beyond and outside of the chemical realm. There is no possibility for objectivity within one perceptual realm.

A chemotactile observer experiences two realms at the same *time*. Each is an entirely distinct experience, but coordinated with the other into a single two-dimensional world. If they were not coordinated, the experience would be of two one-dimensional worlds. The chemotactile world is dimensional, but not spatial: The body in the absence of the higher realms is nonspatial, as we have seen, and there can be no taste perception at a distance from the body. Taste and touch happen in the same nonplace. But they *do* happen in time. Taste is coordinated with touch in the time dimension: Whenever an object is tasted, it is always touched at the same time. The chemical realm of perception corresponds to the time dimension the way the tactile realm corresponds to the second time dimension, or mass.

It is this temporal structure of taste and touch realms that creates the illusion of "something" being tasted and simultaneously touched. Something external appears to be causing these two experiences together. The temporal coordination of separate perceptions of the same "thing" is actually due to the structural interrelation of the time and mass dimensions, but this is not itself perceived directly. The concept of matter has evolved because this structure of consciousness is not immediately experienced. It does not present itself on the chemotactile level any more than on the aural-visual level. In the apparent absence of any other explanation, the concept of matter becomes a convenience. External to each realm, it allegedly causes perceptions within them to coincide. Material substance explains the coordination of sensory realms in a more immediate manner than the dimensional structure of consciousness, the way the geocentric view of the solar system explains what you see when you look up in the sky more immediately than the heliocentric view. The material world arises as a short cut to an understanding of objective experience even on this most rudimentary level. And there it has become entrenched.

That the concept of material substance is a short cut to a full understanding of objective reality is becoming apparent only in the age of relativity theory and quantum mechanics. It has proven a useful concept in getting us from the cell membrane to the early Space Age. But if a dimensional structure of consciousness is a better understanding, as I am suggesting, there should be some evidence or purpose for it outside of physics. There should be some universality to it. Even on the chemotactile level of consciousness there should be some evolutionary advantage to it, some reason why living cells adopt dimensional structures for separate sensory realms and intercoordinate them. As complex chemicals enclose themselves in cells, and cells organize themselves into complex organisms, there must be a reason why this particular route is taken. The evolutionary advantage is, I believe, that of *potential* perception, and therefore, of choice. If an organism experiences actual perception without potential perception, it has no choices. In the case of chemotactile consciousness, what a cell touches it may or may not wish to "taste," or bring in through the cell membrane. It learns through tactile perception what and how and when and where it can assimilate something before committing to do so. Potential chemical sensations built into actual tactile sensations act as a screening mechanism whereby an organism may pick and choose what it eats. The cell enclosure becomes a semipermeable membrane through which only the most desirable objects may pass. This is an enormous biological advantage.

The Spatial Realms

THIS SAME ADVANTAGE RECURS WITH EACH HIGHER REALM OF SENSORY CONSCIOUS-ness. We smell what we potentially taste, and see and hear what we potentially touch. We do not have to commit ourselves until there is some idea of what we are getting into. There is a chance to think about it, and there is some order in what is done. We see something that looks good and can decide whether or not to touch it, or we hear a train coming and can decide whether or not to avoid an unpleasant tactile sensation. Dimensional structure creates potential perception, and potential perception creates the possibility of doing.

But potential perception is also explainable in terms of matter. That is all matter really is. Matter is a more commonsense way of explaining why an object you are seeing is also touchable and hearable. Its drawback is that it requires you to believe in an entire universe of dead substance that you have no way to experience directly. You just have to believe in it. Dimensional correspondence does not ask you to believe anything other than what you see. It states that the reason you can also hear and touch it has nothing to do with the object itself, and everything to do with the space and the time that you see it in.

Space is the living, vibrating essence of higher perceptual consciousness. Dimensional location is where an object is potentially perceived in every realm of consciousness. There is nothing in the object, or in anything else beyond your ability to experience. You see and hear and touch everything that is actually there, and potentially much more. Actual experience is actual existence; the physical reality that you do not experience is potential only. The far side of the moon, and the wall behind your head, do not *actually* exist.

The first perceptual realm corresponding to a space dimension is the olfactory. We smell objects that are not in contact with the body and that are, therefore, in space. If the olfactory were the only realm, the observer would have no way to conceive of an object apart from the perception itself — no more than if there were only a tactile or chemical realm — and there would be no need for space. But the olfactory realm does not exist without the chemo-tactile realms, and space becomes necessary to coordinate it with the other two. Since olfactory information is qualitatively distinct from touch or taste, an entirely new perceptual context is created within which it can be understood apart from them but in conjunction with them. A whole new dimension with a whole new set of possibilities is added to the world. When an observer smells something, it is in a dimension entirely apart from his body, but one to which his body is connected. If he likes what he smells, he can interchange the right space and time dimensions and contact the object. If he does not like it, he can avoid it. He can choose to actualize it or not.

We have all smelled things that we were not sure were "real." Unless you can point to the object you are smelling (see it), you may be accused of smelling the end of your nose. Locating an olfactory object can be quite difficult, even if the sensation is strong. With a *single* olfactory perception it is impossible to know how far away it is, or even what direction it is in. The object exists in three space dimensions in the visual realm but only one in the olfactory. To "find" it you need several time-separated olfactory perceptions. Even without seeing or hearing, you can "sniff around" for a while and locate a gradient, or a path, in which the smell gets stronger. By this means you establish the object's direction. But you still do not know how far away it is: It could be a weak source nearby or a strong source far away. If you follow the gradient long enough, you will bump into the object. It will become actualized in the tactile realm and you can decide whether to actualize it in any other realm. Those of us watching you sniff your way to the object might *see* you going south, then east, and then northeast for forty-nine feet, but if you did not use hearing or seeing, you would have no sense of these other space dimensions. You would only feel your body rotate and accelerate as you interchanged space and time dimensions in conjunction with the olfactory gradient.

With hearing you can locate an object more quickly. A single auditory perception indicates the direction of the source. You can tell which way to go to find it, but you cannot tell how far away it is. You cannot tell if it is a quiet source nearby or a loud source far away, assuming, of course, that you are not using vision. This assumes also that you cannot identify the source — that is, that you do not know from previous experience that the source is a car horn or the neighbor's dog, and cannot thereby judge the distance of the source by the volume of its sound. In real life we do use vision, and we can identify the sources of most of the sounds we hear, so we can usually tell about how far away they are. But a single auditory perception contains implicit information as to direction, but no information as to distance.

Sound consists of longitudinal waves, or successive "crests," of compacted air molecules spread out in two space dimensions interspersed with "troughs" of less compacted air. Like water waves, the crests and troughs of sound waves are arranged in the direction of their propagation. Because the waves are spread out in space, their direction can be determined with the use of two receptors also spread out in space. If you wanted to know the direction of incoming water waves without seeing them, you could stand in the surf with your hands extended on either side and feel which hand touches the waves first. The waves will be coming from that direction. The greater the time differential between the first hand and the second, the greater the angle of incidence. You need both hands to determine this, the way you need both ears to determine the direction of incoming sound waves.

The space dimension corresponding to the auditory realm is constructed from an orderly time sequence of minute tactile sensations on the tympanum, or the eardrum. Each cell on the tympanum can only relay that it has experienced the impact of a small number of air molecules, but the organism as a whole "hears" when many such experiences are relayed in a time-orderly pattern, or wave. The time order becomes a space dimension when a slight time differential is perceivable between one ear and another. It is possible to hear with only one ear, but it takes two ears to take full advantage of the dimensional information implicit in longitudinal waves. (Or at least one large ear: A single receptor sufficiently spread out in space would do.)

Light, the visual realm of consciousness, comes in the form not of longitudinal, but of transverse, waves. Wave "crests" and "troughs" are at right angles to the line of propagation, and carry with them an additional dimension of information. Where each air molecule is only a small part of a relatively large longitudinal sound wave, each photon is its own transverse wave, impacting at a single point. Much more information arrives with each photon than with each air molecule, even though photons have far less energy. The wave of each photon is expressed in terms of its frequency or its "per second" value, which, interestingly, is also the "per second" of the mass dimension. This frequency is perceived as color. Visible photons come in a range of colors from red (low frequency) to violet (high frequency). Visual consciousness consists of points of color in space and time; visual objects are patterns of photons in space–time.

Because sound waves are spread out in space and relatively large compared to most macroscopic objects, they are able to travel around objects in their path. This is why you can hear somebody talking in the next room when you cannot see him. It is difficult to tell relative distances of sound sources because sound waves are not blocked by interposing objects. You can hear a distant sound source even if it is in the exact same direction as a nearer one; there is no "line of sight" blockage. If you cannot see or identify a sound source it is impossible to say how far away it is, even in relative terms. But light waves are at right angles to the line of sight and so compact that nearby objects block more distant ones. You can tell how far away something is relative to something else in the same direction by whether it blocks it or not. Usually you know the approximate distance of visual objects because you can identify them and tell by the size of their visual image about how far away they are, but it is possible to tell relative distances without object identification, and with only one eye. Visual information is, therefore, three-dimensional while auditory information is only two-dimensional. The third space dimension corresponds to the visual realm of consciousness.

Dimensional Correspondence

FOR EACH REALM OF PERCEPTUAL CONSCIOUSNESS THERE IS, THEREFORE, A CORRE-sponding space, time, or mass dimension. I cannot prove that it is true; I can only show that it works. It may be the idea that replaces material substance, or it may not, but I am sure that material substance will be replaced, and I like the way dimensional correspondence looks. It appears complicated because it goes against the grain of established patterns of thinking, but it is ultimately simple. The more you understand it, the simpler it gets. Areas of great complexity boil down to a few axioms. Dimensional correspondence is right, I think, because it is simple.

But what does it mean to say that a dimension "corresponds" to a realm of perception, and what exactly is a dimension? A mental image is a percep-tion only because of its dimensional context. If it is not in a dimension, it is an idea, or a dream, or an illusion, and not a perception. Ideas, dreams, and illusions are as "real" as perceptions; they just don't happen in space. Images that are perceptual come in five varieties, each with a corresponding dimen-sion. These five together make the physical world.

A dimension is an infinite potential for sensory information. It is not actual experience. It is an empty "space," already in the mind, that gives meaning to what is actually perceived. All information has to have context to be meaning-ful. If you just hear someone say, "Fifty-nine," you will have no idea what it means. But if you know that the next number you hear will be the number of home runs Mark McGuire has hit so far and that he has to hit more than sixty-one to break Roger Maris's record, the number fifty-nine will have a context and a meaning. You may get interested, excited even. It is only the context that can cause you to be excited by something as dull as a two-digit number. There can be a different context for the same number. Suppose fifty-nine were the price in dollars for the lunch you just ate. Your reaction would be quite different. A dimension is a context for perceptual experience.

A dimension is the *most fundamental* context of perceptual experience. It is an infinite set of possibilities that *could be* anything other than what they actually are. This is the essential definition of *information*. It has to be some-thing that could be anything else. A telegraph key, for instance, as a source of information, provides a particular sequence of dots and dashes that is the message. But it is information only because the dots and dashes could have come in any other order. "Intelligence" comes through the wire because of the possibilities provided by long and short electrical signals. A black-and-white television screen provides information through patterns of light dots, some of them off and some on. The picture comes to life only because the pattern could be totally random, or "entropic," like the fuzz you see on a channel that has signed off for the night. *Entropy* means lack of order with the potential for order. Information depends on entropy because it depends on the possibility for disorder in order to be orderly. Dimensions are like telegraph keys and television screens except that they are infinite. They range from right here right now to the beginning and end of the universe and everything in it. Anything can happen in dimensions, and that is why we pay particular attention to them.

But why, if there are five sensory realms and five dimensions, do we experience them all together? If there is a separate dimension for each realm, why do we not experience them separately?

If we did, we would experience five separate one-dimensional worlds instead of one multidimensional world. A single multidimensional world requires a special structure. The special structure of the actual physical world is not a random structure and it is not a purely mental, or conceptual, structure. It is derived from actual experience within one of the five perceptual realms, the visual. Because light has so much more capacity for information than the other realms, its structure has become an overall structure for perception. Hearing and touching, etc. are superimposed on the structure of seeing: What we hear and feel we "envision" where we would see it. The space–time within which all perceptual consciousness is experienced is the space and time structure of light. This is why light is not in space–time but space–time in light.

Light

It is no wonder, then, that we should have difficulty finding a physical medium for light, and no wonder that light should behave so strangely "in" space. Looking for light in space is like looking for a house in a room of the house you are looking for. Physicists define a line in space as the path taken by a beam of light; they define space, therefore, in terms of light, at the same time that they try to find light in space! It is this circularity that has exhausted attempts to get at the true nature of light within a materialist worldview.

What, then, is light? Physicists think of it as either waves or particles, but there are problems with either model. If light consists of waves, nobody knows what is doing the waving, and if of particles, they have to be of no size, shape, or mass (even though they have momentum, which is defined in terms of mass), and they have to accelerate from 0 to 300,000,000 meters per second in absolutely no time at all. Furthermore, a photon, because it travels at "the speed of light," experiences no passage of time at all. From its own reference frame, it leaves the Andromeda galaxy, "travels" across 2,000,000 light-years of intergalactic space, and lands in your eye all at exactly the same time. This is difficult to conceive. Physicists keep thinking of light this way for "operational" reasons — that is, they have no other way to think of it, and they have to think of it in some way to get through the day.

It is more accurate to think of light as consciousness itself. It is not a "thing," and it is not "in" anything. The photons "coming from" the Andromeda galaxy are here, now. This does not change anything about what we know of light and its physical properties, only the standpoint from which we appreciate what we know. Ideas like a physical medium for the transmission of light, already nearing extinction, will have to be abandoned completely, as will more modern concepts such as that of light particles bouncing off material objects. The concept of the photon remains, only in modified form. Rather than a shiny little ball streaking through space, the photon is a tiny point of color within the visual realm of consciousness. It is a little "hit" that a cell in the retina "feels" and that we "see." The frequency of each photon as it impacts the retina is proportional to its energy, and is "seen" as its color: Red is the lowest frequency, and violet the highest.

But by virtue of what I have just said, we cannot visualize this as a photon impacting a retinal cell from the outside. Since tactile consciousness is fundamentally nonspatial, the concept of space cannot arise until the "hit" becomes "seeing." The tactile "hit" of the photon is experienced only on its own terms, from "within." Light is, therefore, not "felt" in space in its tactile form. Space arises along with the rise of the visual realm as a context for photon patterns and a means of coordinating vision with the other perceptual realms. Each photon, as it becomes visual, becomes a point in three dimensions of space and one of time.

Visual objects are patterns of many photons, each pattern being a range of points in space–time. The location of each point indicates the location of potential hearing, smell, touch, and taste. But seeing an object at a particular location gives no indication of *actual* information in these realms. You cannot know by seeing the object what it will taste or sound like (unless, of course, you identify it from previous experience), and you cannot tell by the size or shape of the object what it will taste or sound like. Potential perception simply means that at *each point* in the pattern there is the possibility of touch, sound, taste, and smell. In real life very little potential perception is actualized. You rarely hear the cup you see on the shelf, or taste the shingles you hear flapping on the roof. But you know, as well as you can know anything at all, that if you were to climb up the tree in the backyard and stroke your hand where you see a small twig at the middle of a branch, you would feel something at exactly that place. You take it for granted that this is true, and your faith in the order of the universe depends on it absolutely. It is important enough that you should try it occasionally, just to be sure.

If light is not in space–time, how is it that we know its "velocity," c, to be 300,000,000 meters per second? How can it have a velocity if it is not in space? c is stated in terms of "meters per second," as is velocity, but I do not believe that c is a velocity. It is a fundamental constant in the structure of the universe: one second *equals* 300,000,000 meters. One second *is the same thing as c* meters. c is so large a number that we do not notice in everyday life that space comes from time. But it is not an infinite number. If it were infinite, there would be no distortions at dimensional extremes and no relativity theory. Space–time as defined by c is a nearly perfect set of potentials for perceptual consciousness, but not an absolutely perfect one. It looks smooth enough in the house and around the yard, but its rough edges show when you look too far away, go too fast, or look too closely. Because c is so large, space looks like an infinite structure external to light, but the fact that c is not infinite makes it look like a finite velocity in space.

Space and time are also related to mass through Einstein's famous equation stating the fundamental equivalence between mass and energy: $E = mc^2$. This is a fascinating equation for a variety of reasons, one of them having to do with the units in which it is expressed. Mass is always measured in terms of grams, and energy in terms of gram-meters^2 per second^2. But both sides of any equation stating a physical truth have to balance not only in magnitude, but also in terms of units. You cannot have grams equaling meters, even if you have the same number of each. How is it, then, that mass, with a one-dimensional unit, can be the same thing as energy, with a five-dimensional unit? Where do the other four dimensions come from? They come, of course, from the "c^2." This balances the equation nicely on the chalkboard, but how is it that four additional dimensions of space and time suddenly show up in the real world when mass becomes energy?

When a little bit of mass (the "hit" of a photon) *becomes* "seeing," the additional space and time dimensions *are created*. The space–time universe comes into being at that point. Without seeing, the four space–time dimensions we are familiar with do not exist. The context of visual consciousness arises only as vision itself arises, and it is totally separate from the tactile realm. $E = mc^2$ shows that the visual and tactile realms, while entirely separate on the macroscopic level, are fundamentally related on the quantum level. A very small amount of touch, if manipulated into the proper context, can become an enormous quantity of energy in space and time.

The space and time created in the mass-energy conversion are structures of visual consciousness, but also of the universe itself. Space and time, related to mass in terms of c, are derived from the visual realm and imposed on auditory, olfactory, tactile, and chemical realms. The dimensional structure of light becomes the dimensional structure of perceptual consciousness as a whole. We perceive in the nonvisual realms where and when we potentially see. But why light? Could not some other perceptual realm, such as sound, be a universal structure? I believe it could be, but there are reasons why it is not.

If sound were the universal structure, our universe would have two space dimensions instead of three. (With time added, there would be a three-dimensional as opposed to a four-dimensional "space–time.") Visual consciousness might still be possible, but as light is one dimension more complex than sound, four-dimensional visual objects would have to be "foreshortened" into three. The additional dimension would have to manifest itself in each object rather than in the world as a whole. It is impossible to say exactly how this could be done, but it would most likely involve another time dimension. Visual objects in a two-dimensional field would move in more than one time dimension. I suspect this because, in the light-based space–time that we are familiar with, mass is foreshortened as an additional time dimension in each massive object. The mass of an object cannot be directly determined at a single point in time, but only in terms of acceleration, or time per time. Visual objects might behave in sound space the way massive objects behave in visual space. In any case, because photons carry so much more information than air molecules, a lot of information would have to be crammed into sound space. It would be like feeding the information of a written page, or worse, of a video screen, through a telegraph key. Much more time would be required to digest the same amount of information.

The additional space dimension provided by light allows more information through at a given point in time, and that is why it is preferable to sound or any other realm of consciousness as a universal structure. But it is not a perfect structure. Not only is it limited at dimensional extremes, but it is limited in its number of dimensions even though it has more than any other realm. It has one more space dimension than sound, but even three space dimensions can be limiting if additional realms of consciousness are incorporated into its universal structure. Mass, as a fifth dimension corresponding to the tactile realm, already strains light's four-dimensional field. Other realms and corresponding dimensions would have to show up in a light-based world structure as additional time dimensions foreshortened within each object. This would complicate the parameters of motion. There are no such additional *perceptual* realms, but there is at least one additional *observational* realm. Observers possess a time dimension additional even to that of mass. They move in ways that merely massive objects do not and further strain light's capacity as a universal dimensional structure.

But how is it that the structure of light becomes the structure of the universe itself? The answer is in the structural relation between what I have called the photon screen and the quantum screen. The photon screen is like a three-dimensional television screen. Most such screens are, of course, two-dimensional, so we have to imagine the "depth" (the space dimension that is foreshortened on an actual television screen). Each point on the screen is a photon. Each photon is a particular color, and exists at a particular point in three dimensions of space and one of time. Physical objects are patterns of photons on the screen. The quantum screen is a model for perceptual consciousness as a whole. It is the same thing as the photon screen except that it extends infinitely in all directions beyond actual vision, and includes all five sensory realms. What you touch in the dark, or behind your back, is on the quantum screen but not on the photon screen. It is not actually visible, only potentially so, right where you feel it. Each quantum on the screen is a point in five dimensions: three in space and two in time. The photon screen is the visible portion of the quantum screen. If a quantum is actualized in the form of light (you turn the lights on, or look in the direction of a sound), its second time dimension becomes the photon's frequency, or color.

The quantum screen is, therefore, an extrapolation of the photon screen. Its structure is based on that of actual vision. It is nowhere "in" space or time in that it defines space and time. The quantum screen is an extrapolation of the photon screen in the same way that a single quantum is an extrapolation of a single photon. We see a photon as a point in space–time, and we see, hear, smell, touch, or taste a quantum as a point in space–time–time. It should be noted, however, that we experience *aggregates* of quanta in nonvisual realms and not *individual* quanta. They are too small to hear, smell, or taste individually.

Physicists normally think of a photon as a type of quantum because quanta, as basic units of energy, can exist in nonphoton form, and only sometimes reveal themselves as units of light energy. But *single* quanta do not reveal themselves except as photons. There is no actual perception of individual quanta except as photons. Individual quanta, then, are abstractions based on actual experience with photons and are best described as "potential photons," in that they do not exist in any other form. Collectively, of course, quanta can be experienced as nonlight energy. Air molecules impacting the tympanum, for instance, each consist of many billions of quanta.

The Western mind does not know what to do with the quantum. Is it material? Is it a "little ball" of energy? We know that it is the smallest unit of energy, but energy can be converted into mass (matter), so it must be something more fundamental than matter, even though there is nothing more fundamental than matter. Sometimes we try to understand quanta as particles, sometimes as increments of space and time. That they are mysterious is all we can say, and that they do not fit into our world. But if we understand the quantum as a point at which a unit of tactile experience becomes a unit of vision, we can see it as the beginning of the differentiation of consciousness into separate realms, and the origin of corresponding space dimensions. It does not fit into our world because it is the world.

The quantum screen is a particularly good model of this world in that each quantum, though extremely small in itself, is not infinitely small. There are tiny "spaces" in between individual points, as there are tiny spaces between individual lights on a television screen. There is a certain "graininess," therefore, to physical reality that shows up on the quantum level as de Broglie waves or as the Heisenberg Uncertainty Principle. Physical objects are patterns of quanta, in the way that objects on a television screen are patterns of little lights. As long as objects are fairly large, the graininess is not noticed, but when objects become small relative to the individual quanta of which they consist, the graininess shows. Similarly, when objects on a television screen become as small as the individual lights of the screen itself, they lose their dimensional definition. You cannot have a pattern of quanta smaller than an individual quantum. Extremely small objects, like electrons, appear to "jump" between one quantum and another the way an extremely small object on television could only be seen jumping from one tiny light to another. This is how the quantum screen explains the discoveries of quantum mechanics.

The quantum screen is also limited by the fact that space and time are fundamentally related to each other by the constant c, and both are related to mass by c^2. Patterns cannot move on the screen faster than c because, due to the structure of the screen itself, you cannot fit any more than c meters in a second. If you try to do so, the extra meters will end up in the mass dimension. Patterns approaching c meters per second end up becoming more massive instead of faster. The quantum screen is more than adequate for everyday life on the macroscopic level but reveals inherent limitations when patterns on the screen become dimensionally larger or smaller than the screen itself. This is how the quantum screen explains the findings of relativity theory.

But there is a twist to the use of light as a universal structure. I said earlier that tactile consciousness in the absence of other perceptual realms is fundamentally *nonspatial*, in that it is impossible to experience anything at a distance from the body if the body is all that is experienced. The body, in the absence of specialized sensory organs, is the world itself. I also said that other sensory realms, particularly vision, are reducible to tactile sensation. Tactile consciousness is, therefore, more fundamental than visual. But I am saying here that tactile consciousness is coordinated with vision *in terms of vision*! We touch something where we potentially see it, even though seeing itself is fundamentally a form of touch. This is not as contradictory as it sounds, but it requires a re-examination of just how the tactile realm is experienced.

Tactile consciousness is experienced as either unquantized or quantized — in either nonspatial or spatial form. Usually things are felt as if they were located on the screen, but the screen is not *needed* to feel things, only to coordinate what is felt with what is seen. In the absence of other realms, tactile consciousness is experienced as unquantized and nonspatial. Unicellular organisms experience tactile stimuli in this way, as do multicellular organisms without sensory organs. In hatha yoga it is possible to experience the body as the whole world rather than as a shape in a larger spatial world. This type of yoga is, perhaps, a conscious suspension of the quantum screen. More commonly, the tactile realm is experienced in quantized form — that is, as a pattern of actualized quanta in space and time coordinated with vision, and thereby with sound, taste, and smell. The body becomes a mobile pattern on the quantum screen. Even here, tactile consciousness is not in space but takes a rectilinear, or "right angle," relation to the whole of space–time as a second time dimension. In this way the tactile realm and acceleration become the same thing.

The quantization of tactile consciousness is, therefore, the projection of an abstract structure onto a fundamentally nonspatial realm of consciousness. It occurs only when light arises as a separate perceptual realm, in order to coordinate five perceptual realms into a single, integrated dimensional world. The quantum screen arises on a very fundamental level as a projection of the body. The body then cuts loose from its nonspatial origins, and jumps onto the screen as a shape in space–time–time.

Other People

THE QUANTUM SCREEN IS A COMPLETE PICTURE OF PERCEPTUAL CONSCIOUSNESS. Everything that I see, hear, smell, taste, and touch is on the screen. Space and time are the screen itself. If there were but one person, this would be the entirety of the physical world. But there are other people in the world, and there are apparently other consciousnesses in other people. If consciousness is not "in" space and time, as I have said, why is it that other people are in space and time? Are they not truly conscious? Am I the only true "being"?

If there are *other* beings "in" the world, human and otherwise, consciousness is in space and time, and the idea I am suggesting is wrong. But how could it be otherwise? Other people are on the quantum screen, and therefore in space and time. Where else could their consciousnesses be? And when they say they see and hear the things I see and hear, how can this be explained except in terms of a world whose existence depends on neither my consciousness nor theirs? How could the world be "my" consciousness with other people in it who see it too?

This is a big question, and one on which immaterialist theories have had a great deal of difficulty. The nonexistence of matter seems to imply solipsism, a rather distasteful notion that everything is "me." If physical reality has no existence outside of consciousness, everything has to be in consciousness, including other consciousnesses. This is an absurdity. Who gets to have the "real" consciousness, you or I? There is no comfortable answer to this question, and no convincing one. It is an ugly question, and one that has been avoided, even in the face of an overwhelming physical need to ask it. It seems that we cannot question that tables and chairs are "out there" without questioning that "you" are out there, apart from me. Tables and chairs are physically doubtful, but *meta*physically essential to maintain the separate identities of our selves. But deciding between "you" and "me" is the wrong question. If consciousness is something that neither you nor I "have," there may be a better question, and a better answer.

And this is the importance of the discussion at hand. The existence of matter is secondary. The relation between you and me and people down the block and plants and animals all over the earth is what makes modern physics so crucial. It is a question of being. Quarks and black holes and the speed of light are interesting and important in their own right, but their significance at this point in the development of human civilization goes far beyond their scientific value. They are telling us something about ourselves, something more than a vague, esoteric connectedness. Quantum mechanics and relativity theory look like complicated puzzles for men in white lab coats to play with, but they are far more. They are a major turning point in the development of civilization and will transform all aspects of human life. They will transform being. As we find out what they mean, we will become something other than what we think we are, and new myth will arise. Quantum mechanics and relativity theory will force the question. The answer is who we become.

Let us look more closely at the question. The quantum screen is the whole of *perceptual* consciousness, but not the whole of consciousness. Other people seem to have a reality to their existence that is more than what "I" perceive, and more than just the quantum screen, yet everything I know of other people comes through one perceptual realm or another, and therefore through the quantum screen. Other people are at the same time "in" and "more than" perceptual consciousness. How is this possible? The answer is in the particular nature of the perceptual experience by which I am aware of other people.

This experience differs from other perceptual experience in two important ways. First, it is highly *ordered*. The sounds that I hear coming from other people's mouths, and the shapes that I see them writing on paper, are so highly arranged as to make me believe that they "have" perceptual consciousness more or less equivalent to my own. And second, it comes in the form of *potential perception*. Everything other people say they see is what I can see directly, if I choose to look. They have to be telling the truth, of course, and I may have to go where they are in space and time to see what they say they see, but there is a definite *dimensional* coordination between information from "observers" (other people) and direct perceptual experience. It is *the same* dimensional structure that exists between each of the five perceptual realms of consciousness, except that information from other people is potential perception *as a whole*. Other people are both "in" and "more than" perceptual consciousness because they constitute an entirely separate realm of consciousness that is *reducible* to perceptual experience. The "observational realm" is a wholeness over and above the separate perceptual parts by which it is made known. It is made from its perceptual parts the same way that vision is made from its tactile parts. Observational information is highly ordered hearing and seeing, but it is also a separate reality unto itself.

Where the photon screen is a model for visual consciousness, and the quantum screen for perceptual consciousness as a whole, the "image screen" becomes a model for observational consciousness. When somebody tells you about something that is happening on the other side of town, you experience it on the image screen. You do not see or hear it directly, only potentially, but it has a dimensional location. The image screen has the same structure as the quantum screen, and often coincides with it, as when you happen to see something at the same time that someone else describes it. As the image screen is a model for potential perceptual consciousness as a whole, it is the same thing as the physical universe.

I do not experience directly what observers say they see and hear and touch. There is no *actual* perceptual consciousness in their description. If we define "reality" as "actual experience," there is no reality to *their* actual seeing, hearing, and touching. If we define *reality* as "potential or actual experience" their experience is as real as my own. Other people are not, then, other consciousnesses, but sources of observational information. (As am I, when I communicate perceptual experience.) "I" am a pivot between perception and observation: What "I" perceive directly is a "slice" of a much greater whole. Most of what I know about the world is through other people rather than through direct perceptual experience, and as technology advances, I perceive less and less on my own. Observation is not more real than perception, but it is a greater reality in that there is so much more to it. It is a much larger world. Observation is what anybody, anywhere can perceive at anytime, and therefore the world we know through science.

Observational consciousness is not "in" me or "in" observers, but something that transcends individual objects and people. It is larger than the limited perceptual world that I see and hear and touch, and manifests itself on the quantum screen only in terms of "order." It is the physical order of sound waves in a communicated message, of letters on a page, of a clean kitchen, or of a well-designed building. The order I see in human creations all around me, and even of nonhuman living things, is merely a cross-section of observational consciousness. It is only that part of a much greater whole that can be squeezed onto the quantum screen, in foreshortened form.

Observers create observational consciousness the way retinal cells create visual consciousness. Observers see or hear directly, then communicate information based on this perceptual experience in a form that is potentially perceivable by other observers. Retinal cells take direct tactile experience and create vision, communicating information in a form that is potential tactile experience to other cells in the body. Other cells know what the information means, and can decide what to do about it, because the experience is potential and not actual. The predator across the meadow need not be touched directly to be experienced. This is the value of visual information to other cells. The value of observational information to other individual people is that it indicates what can be perceived directly, but need not be. I don't have to go to Antarctica to know that it is cold there because other people have told me that it is. I do not have to feel actual cold to know that it exists. But the value of vision to nonretinal cells, or of observational information to other people, is not the full dynamic of visual or observational consciousness. Vision creates a multicellular wholeness, and observation a collective human consciousness. We, as observers, are in the process of creating a human wholeness far greater than ourselves individually.

As perceivers, however, you and I are still dependent on the quantum screen. I see you on the screen, and hear you on the screen telling me you see me on "your" screen. The "reality" of your screen to me, or of mine to you, is a matter of potential experience only. We will have to settle for that, since there is only one consciousness. I often think of it as "mine," but I am learning and trying, through the process of living, to grow larger than self. All of the great spiritual and literary traditions point you and me in this direction, and we know that it is a truth. You and I feel some things directly and other things only through each other. We are physically separate and metaphysically whole. I feel your pain because I would feel it in your situation. It is real pain, tactile or observational, actual or potential, through the body or through a certain order of quanta. It is pain, and that is what creates humanity.

You and other observers show up on the quantum screen the way other physical objects do, but you move differently. You are capable of a type of motion that tables and chairs and other inanimate objects are not. They move with constant velocity, or with constant acceleration, but unlike you, they cannot *change acceleration* in an orderly manner. They bounce off whatever is in their way, while you move around things so as not to collide with them. Their motion is predictable and yours is not. If I know the position and momentum of inanimate objects at any given time within a closed system, I can know their position and momentum at any other time, past or future (within the limits of quantum uncertainty, of course), but I cannot say which way you, or any other observer, will turn when you leave the room. The fact that you are an observer means that there is a sort of *macroscopic* uncertainty to your behavior. (Despite the uncertainty, there are *probabilities* associated with your behavior, as there are with quantum particles.) Inanimate objects change the direction and magnitude of their velocities only when acted on by external forces, but you are able to do so on your own.

Does this mean that there is another dimension — a third time dimension, perhaps, corresponding to the observational realm of consciousness — that appears foreshortened on the quantum screen? If so, it is not quite the same as the others. The main difference is that it is not measurable. It is plain that there are degrees of "order," ranging from the writhing motion of common earthworms, through the nest building of songbirds, to romantic poetry, but there is no way that we know of to quantify it. There is an inverse relation between order and probability (the more orderly a system, the less probable), but there is no means to assign a distinct numerical value to it. It is not like meters and seconds and kilograms in this respect. It is like a dimension in that it represents potential perception. Every point in space or time is a point of potential perception; either it is empty or it is occupied with a physical object. At every point where there is orderly nonuniform acceleration (an observer), there is an entire universe of potential perception. Each potential universe that is an observer is in space–time, but that universe, as infinite as it may be, does not interfere in any way with space or time (or mass). It is at a sort of rectilinear (right-angle) relation to space–time–mass as a whole. Each observer is like a "wormhole" or a "hyperlink" through direct perceptual consciousness to a larger dimensional world.

I am part of that larger world only if I communicate. To experience observational consciousness passively, I need only listen to what other people say. To contribute to it, however, I must convert perceptual experience into observational information by structuring it into a potentially perceivable form. *I must do something that becomes being.* I must make sounds or create symbols that are ordered in such a way that actual perception becomes potential perception.

Other observers have to be able to see what I say I see. I must, therefore, say what I see, as I see it, even if it is not in my self-interest. I must not lie, omit, or exaggerate. The self, associated with perceptual consciousness, must be subverted for the sake of a higher consciousness and a higher self. I am a good observer to the extent that I am articulate and honest. It is by these virtues that civil society is constructed.

THE DIMENSIONAL STRUCTURE OF CONSCIOUSNESS IS BASED ON A NEW DEFINITION of reality that includes all experience — subjective and objective, perceptual and conceptual — and on the fundamental assumption that each realm of perceptual consciousness corresponds to a space or time dimension. It explains new experience that human beings have had at extremes of space, time, and mass. It has made itself necessary because of these experiences. It will create new myth that changes who we are in relation to other living things and to ourselves. With this there is hope.

Chapter 7

Meditation

MEDITATION IS TRYING TO DO BEING AND IT CANNOT BE DONE. THE SECOND step is to know this, the first is to do it anyway.

The practice of meditation is extremely simple and extremely difficult. All you do is allow awareness to present itself, take it in, and let go. Look at what is. Do not keep anything. You can sit on the floor or in a chair, or stand on the street corner waiting for a bus. You can watch your breathing, or your thoughts, feel your aches and pains, listen to sounds, or recite a mantra if you have one. Traditions, beliefs, positions, mantras, and spiritual guidance are absolutely essential and of no consequence. It is very difficult to get anywhere without them. Going it on your own is like swimming the ocean. You need a vessel. But you do not need anything at all.

Meditation will not do you any good. There is nothing in it for you. If it makes you happier, it may also make you sadder. If it makes you healthier, it may also make you tired, or bored, or boring. It is not exciting. If it makes you see wonderful things about yourself and the world and the nature of being, you have to let them go. What you experience does not last and you will never see it again. There is no point to it. You cannot talk about what you experience except in the most oblique and hollow manner that will sound shallow even to yourself. You may experience nothing. You will probably experience nothing. If you do not experience nothing you have not done the not doing that you are trying to do. I recommend it to no one. If you do it anyway, be prepared to fail. Failure and frustration are important.

MEDITATION IS *BEING* WITHOUT *SELF*. THAT IS WHY YOU CANNOT DO IT.

Chapter 8

Becoming

Being a Cell

WHAT WE KNOW OF LIFE ON THE CELLULAR LEVEL WE KNOW FROM A MULTI-cellular perspective. We see and understand cellular life in terms of shape and motion in space. But this is to misunderstand *being* a cell. Cells do not see and hear and smell and do not, therefore, experience space. Their perceptual consciousness is limited to the chemical and tactile realms, or to what we as multicellular beings experience in the form of taste and touch. We cannot know the actual experience of an individual cell, but the dimensional structure of its world is what we would experience if we were able to limit own experience to these two realms. If it were possible to neither see nor hear nor smell, and to have never seen nor heard nor smelled, and never communicated with anyone who had, we would experience the same dimensional structure experienced by individual cells. Our perceptual world would be structured only in time dimensions.

We can know this world. It is difficult to experience directly because it is difficult to ignore the far greater part of our perceptual experience that is spatial, our memories thereof, and what we may know through the spatial experience of others. But we do experience the same types of perceptions that are experienced by individual cells. We can highlight actual experience within the chemical and tactile realms and extrapolate from it a sense of what it is like to be a cell. We are, after all, composed of cells. Our own being is over and above the being of individual cells within us, but all of our experience is, or is derived from, cellular experience. Let us look, then, within the structure of the chemotactile world.

The chemical realm is more fundamental than the tactile. It predates even the cell itself. But we experience it even now through the biochemistry of taste and digestion. Acids, for example, are experienced in the form of a sour taste, and sugars through the more pleasant sensation of sweetness. This is the actual, direct chemical experience of some of our cells, as communicated to the rest of them. There is no way to know if cells in our tongues and stomach linings experience sour and sweet the way we do, and I am sure that their own chemical experience is far more complex and elaborate than what they relay on to the central nervous system, but what they do pass on is a window, however small, into their being. Sourness and sweetness are how well and in what form chemicals within our tasting cells have bonded with dissolved molecules in the environment around them. This is a small "taste" of what it is like to be a cell, or even to be a molecule within a cell. It is less a direct than a translated experience, but remains nonetheless available to us after a billion years of biological evolution.

The actual experience of individual cells is less important to my purpose than the dimensional structure within which it is experienced. From a multi-cellular perspective, chemical sensations are placed in a spatial context — that is, at specific locations in the mouth and gut — but I do not believe that space is intrinsic to chemical perception itself. Because individual cells have to be *in contact* with what they experience chemically, they can have no sense of the existence, or potential existence, of "objects" with which they are not in contact. They can have no sense of "object" as something "out there," wait-ing to be tasted or touched. Either they experience the actual sensation or they do not. There can be no sense of existence "outside" of actual perception. Even the concept of "contact" is a spatial concept that we, who are able to see and hear and smell, impose on a nonspatial world. Objects that *we* may see in the space immediately around but not in contact with a cell do not exist at all for the cell. They are not in its world. Objects not in contact with us that we could not see or hear or smell would not be part of our world either. Space evolves as a context only for multicellular perceptual information, and is not a context for being, unicellular or multicellular.

Neither is it a context for tactile perception. Objects are *seen* in space bouncing off individual cells or off our own bodies for that matter but they are not *felt* in space. They are felt only when they are in contact. When they are not in contact they do not exist in the tactile universe. The concept of "in contact" is, in fact, none other than that of the tactile realm of consciousness as a whole, artificially placed in spatial context. The tactile realm of conscious-ness (the body), *as a shape in space*, is a later adaptation of multicellular con-sciousness. Individual cells do not feel things in space and there can be no question of the existence of anything not in contact. If there is no contact, there is no perception and no object in space waiting to be perceived. Not only is there no object in space, there is no spatial universe "outside" of the body of the cell. There is no experience beyond the cell membrane and no possibility for experience beyond the cell membrane. The cell is, therefore, its own universe. There is no difference between "self" and "world."

It is possible for us, even as multicellular organisms, to experience tactile consciousness nonspatially. It is difficult, as one must again set aside visual, auditory, and olfactory perception, and any memory of or communication about experience in these realms. It can be done through concentration on actual tactile perception (the body) from within — that is, through actively cultivating awareness of sensations throughout various parts of the body without imposing over them any sort of spatial context. There are Eastern meditative traditions that attempt this. Feelings in one arm or leg are "looked at" as they arise in the mind without thinking of them as "on the other side of the body" from the other arm or leg. This way may seem a contrivance, in that we are showing that tactile consciousness is nonspatial by perceiving it nonspatially, but I believe that tactile consciousness can be perceived this way only because it is fundamentally nonspatial. We are merely trying to not see something that is not there. Each sensation of an object in contact with the body is perceived exactly as it is, without thinking of it in space where it *would be seen*. Space is needed to coordinate chemotactile perception with the "higher," multicellular realms of perception, such as vision, but not needed for chemotactile consciousness itself. There is, of course, nothing incorrect about feeling an object in space where it would be seen, but such coordination is unnecessary for a structure of consciousness that predates vision.

Why is structure necessary for chemotactile consciousness, and of what does that structure consist? The structure is necessary because tactile perception is qualitatively distinct from chemical, and the two must be coordinated into a single "world." Each is experienced within a time dimension, and the two realms are intercoordinated in time. An object that is perceived in the chemical realm is perceived in the tactile realm *at the same time*. It is from this intercoordination that the concept of "object" is derived. Each perception in the absence of the other is just a perception and not an object, and there is no sense of there being anything external to consciousness. But when there are perceptions in both realms at the same time it begins to appear as though there is something "out there" causing each to happen, even if it is "out there" in time and not in space.

The distinction between chemical and tactile perception that makes structure necessary arises with the enclosure of biochemical processes within a membrane. There are obvious physiological advantages to a membrane — protection, the availability and concentration of nutrients, etc. — but the enclosure cannot cut the cell off from all contact with the outside. Wastes must be allowed out and nutrients allowed in, and there must remain a means of sensing what types of molecules should be given passage. Cells have evolved a way of "feeling" external molecules through changes in potassium ion concentrations on the membrane itself. This tactile sensation is actually a special quality of chemical sensation. The cell "knows" that there is something fundamentally distinct about this type of chemical sensation and does not put it in the same category as other chemical sensations that it experiences *within* the cell membrane. Tactile sensations are *reducible* to chemical sensations, but they are so fundamentally distinct in how they are perceived and in what they mean to the functioning and survival of the cell that a whole new realm of consciousness is created within which to appreciate them. This new realm of consciousness is the body of the cell. It is also our own body. It is *seen*, from the outside, as a shape in space, but from within, the body is tactile consciousness itself.

The tactile realm is quite literally a whole new dimension added to the universe of cellular being. A new infinity of possibilities arises once an entirely separate category of experience is established. The new category may or may not contain *actual* experience. It could be nearly or entirely empty. As a realm of consciousness, it is a context for a particular type of perceptual experience and not the experience itself. It is the file folder and not the information within the folder.

The being of a cell has two major file folders: one for chemical experience and one for tactile experience. Each has a time dimension associated with it. But it may have other, less defined file folders as well. A folder, or category, and eventually a dimensional potential arise through what may best be called "order." Order is a category of sameness in more than one experience. Most of what the cell experiences in the tactile realm will be random collisions with particles and other cells, but it may from time to time sense a certain regularity to some of these collisions. To manage sensory experience a cell has to create a filing system to store and retrieve data. As soon as one experience becomes more "like" another, the "likeness" takes on a life of its own, and becomes as real as separate experiences within it. A particular tactile or chemical sensation may be categorized as "food," "nonfood," "danger," etc., so that the cell does not have to reexperience what each sensation means every time it senses it. A category that spans more than one sensory realm becomes a physical object, and is experienced in a dimensionally coordinated manner. The cell "tastes" an object at the same time that it "touches" it. The structure of consciousness both within and between sensory realms is based on this system. Only the largest and most fundamental of filing categories becomes a sensory potential, and a sensory potential becomes a dimension only when it is coordinated with other sensory potentials.

The cell may experience order in the form of a vibration, or a series of regularly repeated collisions that take on a recognizable pattern. It may be a pattern similar to one that the cell has experienced within its membrane — that is, something like itself. It has no sense of space, and cannot "envision" another cell "out there" alongside it, but it learns through interpreting tactile patterns to recognize selves other than itself. It learns to avoid not only undesirable molecules in its environment, but other forms of life that are undesirable, or dangerous. And it learns to recognize and eventually associate itself with cells similar to itself.

If this seems too anthropomorphic, too much like cells and organic molecules tasting and touching their way through the primordial soup, it is not because cells and molecules do not actually experience and think about things, it is because in attempting to relate our own being to theirs we have to use what is familiar to us. We must apply the tools we know how to use. But some tools are appropriate and others not. Our sense of taste is appropriate because it is derived from the actual molecular experience of living cells. There really are living beings within our bodies chemically interacting with external substances and relaying that experience on to the body as a whole. We experience this directly. We experience what they relay to us as "taste," and through the medium of this experience we gain a glimpse of what it is like to be a cell. What should not be used are tools appropriate to multicellular experience. It is perhaps necessary for us to "envision" the enclosure of organic molecules "within" a membrane, but this is not what a cell experiences. It can tell the difference a membrane makes, but only in terms of a new realm of consciousness based on the orderly flow of potassium ions.

Neither should we be disturbed by the thought of a cell "feeling," "experiencing," or "knowing." It is true that we cannot see a cell doing any of these things, and we do not know "where" or "how" it could possibly do so, but this is my point. Its being is not in space and cannot be perceived any more than can our own. We do not, after all, see each other feeling or experiencing or knowing. All we see is orderly behavior that seems to indicate that we do. "We" are the composite experience of our cells; we experience because they do.

We know much more about cells, however, than what we touch or taste of them. We know how they metabolize, how they photosynthesize and respire, how they synthesize proteins and reproduce themselves. But this is what they do and not what they are. When we study them only from the outside and know only what they do, we do not know the world that each of them is. It is a large part of the same world known to multicellular beings; to this extent we are what a cell is. Their being is our being.

Being a Multicellular Organism

CELLS THAT UNITE TO FORM COMPLEX CELL COMMUNITIES EITHER DEVELOP AN expanded consciousness within the temporal structure that they know or evolve an entirely new structure of consciousness. Those that become plants remain exclusively chemotactile; they do not develop sensory organs capable of perceiving objects with which they are not in contact. Animal cell communities, on the other hand, evolve specialized sensory cells that perceive chemical or tactile stimuli in a highly ordered form and communicate what they perceive to other cells in the same organism. The cells themselves remain chemotactile, but the experience they encode and relate to each other becomes a higher order of consciousness. Space is the context within which this new intercellular information is encoded.

We can have only the vaguest sense of what it is like to be a plant. There is a degree of communication among plant cells, and an overall sense among them of the adequacy of moisture, light, nutrients, and temperature, but there can be no sense of a world beyond the body of the plant itself. The only possible context for intercellular communication is time. A plant has to be able to detect trends. It cannot know whether to grow, to flower, or to bear fruit unless it knows that water and soil nutrients are increasingly available or that the days are becoming longer or warmer. If there is a sudden cold spell, or a drought, it will know to save its energy until trends improve. A plant, therefore, must be able to make decisions; it must *do* things, however limited its range of choices. Plants of a given species grow and reproduce the same way, but some individuals within that species may begin sooner than others. *What* it does is already programmed into its genetic code; the only choice it has is *when*. The doing that the plant does is, therefore, limited to the release or nonrelease of auxins and other hormones at a given moment. Its range of possibilities, or the *potential* within which it chooses to do, is purely temporal. Its actual experiences and decisions may be anything, but the dimensional structure of its world is the same as that of an individual cell. There is a wholeness to the life of a plant over and above the cells within it, but the structural quality of this wholeness is not distinct from its separate parts. Being a plant is structurally the same as being a cell.

A plant may decide to grow in one part of its body as opposed to another, but this is not a decision based on spatial perception. A tree, for instance, will accelerate growth in branches that experience sunlight and stop growth in those that do not, but it does not perceive either branch pushing out into an emptiness. It can only sense that some of its cells are doing well and others are not, and that the tree as a whole would benefit from choosing the former in its decisions regarding continued growth. We may think that the tree is "really" growing into empty space, but the reality we perceive is based on our structure of consciousness and not its own. It may be argued that a plant senses space within its body if not without, but I do not see how this is possible without experience in the higher sensory realms. Animals learn to perceive their bodies in space, but only in order to coordinate chemotactile consciousness with the higher senses. Space is imposed after the fact. I believe this because, where the higher realms require space, it is possible to experience the chemotactile realms with or without it.

We may also see the tree growing "toward" the light. It is true that the tree senses light and reacts by stimulating growth among those cells that sense it, but it does not experience light as information, the way we do. Light is energy and warmth, but not vision. A tree, or any plant, feels light much the way the cells in our skin feel it, but unlike those in our retinas. The "dual nature of light" is due to the fact that we, as higher animals, are able to both feel and see it.

Being an animal is structurally different from being a plant or a cell. Where a plant's world is much like that of its constituent cells, an animal's world is entirely distinct from its cells because the quality of its perceptual consciousness cannot be experienced by them individually. A plant cell can sense moisture, temperature, or light as can the plant as a whole, but an animal cell cannot see, hear, or smell as can the animal as a whole. The wholeness of animal being is thereby greater than the wholeness of plant being. But how does this arise from the being of individual animal cells?

Where a plant cell feels only heat, a retinal cell in an animal's eye is able to feel what it interprets as an individual photon. By itself this experience is meaningless. It is only when combined with the experience of other retinal cells that information is created, and it is only when this information is organized in a manner that is meaningful and useful to nonretinal cells that visual consciousness is created. A series of retinal experiences becomes vision only when it is a *pattern* that says something to cells in the stomach lining and the muscles of the lower leg. The pattern has to say something about the potential experience of nonretinal cells — something that may affect their need to expand or contract, or to secrete or stop secreting. To become such a pattern the combined experience of the retinal cells must be arranged in an order that all cells throughout the body already understand. The actual retinal experience may be anything, but the order into which it is arranged to create the pattern must be understood beforehand. In other words, there must be a preexisting *potential*, or combination of potentials, into which the pattern fits in order for the information to have meaning. A random series of retinal experiences will tell the stomach lining nothing.

The actual experience of each retinal cell is limited to the frequency, or color, of the photon it feels. The concept of space arises by the arrangement into a pattern of many retinal cell experiences. (It is tempting to think of the pattern arising by the location of each cell in the retina, but this is to put the cart before the horse; our concept of their having "location" in the retina arises from the pattern.) Space, therefore, is not actual visual experience; it is merely the potential (or potentials) into which retinal information is arranged. Space is not actually seen; what is seen are points of color arranged in space. The patterns they create are physical (but not material) objects. We "see" what our retinal cells feel, but only as interpreted by the other cells in our body. Empty space is the wholeness of intercellular being. It is the "consciousness" associated with being an animal. This intercellular consciousness is necessarily limited by the structural limitations of space itself; we can see no objects or patterns smaller than the single photons experienced by single cells. Below this "quantum level," space is not distinguishable from time or mass.

How do individual cells create the order that becomes space? In the case of olfactory information, cell communities develop the first space dimension to distinguish what is actually perceived (the information itself) from the object of perception. With olfactory consciousness, the actual chemical experience of a few molecules assimilated by a few cells in the olfactory organ becomes an "object" with which the organism is not in tactile contact — that is, an object that is "elsewhere" in space. The concept of space is created from the coordination of *actual* sensation of the sensory cells with *potential* sensation of the other cells in the organism. When it smells something, the organism knows that there is something out there beyond its skin that could become chemical or tactile perception. The few molecules actually experienced become information arranged in a spatial pattern as soon as they mean that the organism may expect associated chemotactile experiences at some point in the future. It may eat, or be eaten by, "what" it smells, "out there," even though the "what" is "no more than" an arrangement of actual chemical experiences by a few cells in its nose.

Space means potential experience in the passive sense, but also the possibility of doing. When an organism smells something, it may choose to perceive or to avoid perceiving it in other realms. If it wants to touch or taste, or does not want to touch or taste (or be tasted by), the object it smells, it may take appropriate action. But which way to move becomes a problem. Once the organism identifies the object, it can detect its direction (and thereby determine which way to move) only through future olfactory experience. It cannot know "where" in space the object is until it moves one way and then another, and compares several time-separated olfactory experiences. (It might accomplish the same thing by standing still in a moving medium such as a wind or water current.) If the olfactory information becomes more intense through time, it is moving toward the object, and if less intense, away from it. In any case, the object becomes meaningful as potential perception, and the potential within which it exists creates doing in space as well as doing in time. But this smelling and doing in space is specific to animals; a plant could not benefit from smelling because, even if it were to detect potential nutrition or danger with which it was not in contact, it could do nothing about it.

The second space dimension, associated with hearing, is created from a temporal sequence. Sound arrives on the tympanic membrane in waves, or in a series of *repeated* patterns. Actual auditory experience is reducible to the tactile perceptions of individual tympanic or cochlear cells, but like other forms of perceptual experience, it becomes meaningful to the rest of the organism only when arranged in an orderly pattern. Auditory information is more orderly than olfactory in that it is arranged in two space dimensions. An auditory object is identified not so much by the similarity of one tactile pattern on the tympanum to another previously experienced pattern, but by the similarity of one *wave* of patterns to another previously experienced wave. The temporal order implicit in sound waves becomes a second space dimension in that it is through slight changes within this order that the direction of an auditory object is determined. Direction can be determined immediately because incoming sound waves strike a tympanum in one ear before the other. The minute time differences between tactile perceptions from the same incoming wave crest create the sense of direction and thus of another dimension in space. This new dimension is manifest in the arrangement of auditory information and not in its content; the direction of an auditory object is implicit in the medium of sound transmission and not in actual sounds that are heard.

Because each cell in the organism experiences *the same* orderly patterns of olfactory and auditory information, smelling and hearing can be understood as intercellular media. All cells in the organism can "read" what certain of them have experienced, once it is "written" in spatial patterns. The fact that all cells are "reading" the same information at the same time creates a common experience that is the being of the organism as a whole. Space creates a uniformity of cellular experience.

But in what sense does the actual experience of a few cells in the ears and nose become the "potential" experience of other cells in an organism? All cells require nutrition and protection, and hearing and smelling provide neither. What they do provide is knowledge of where and when there is the possibility of nutrition and danger. The spatial arrangement of perceptual information in either the auditory or olfactory realm indicates where and when there is potential perception in the other. The direction an animal hears its prey is where it may be smelled, and the smell of a predator indicates when to listen for it. But more important for individual cells is that auditory and olfactory information is also dimensionally coordinated with the chemical and tactile realms, the realms they experience directly. Where and when an object is smelled and heard is also where and when it may be touched or tasted. This is what is meant by "potential experience." The spatial arrangement of the actual experience of a few sensory cells indicates the possibility of food and protection for all cells. It does not tell the organism what to do, only where and when it may be done. It is a knowledge that is in the *context* of perceptual information and not in its content; the animal may or may not identify *what* it hears, but it knows from its location in space where it can smell, touch, or taste it.

To extend the analogy of a computer screen, an animal touching something it sees, or listening for something it smells, is "clicking" on an object in one realm on the quantum screen in order to perceive it in another. There are five perceptual "files," some open and others closed, some empty and others full. The "object" exists only as a link between one file and the others. *What* is perceived in any realm has nothing to do with what is perceived in any other; the connection is only in terms of where and when. Each file is at "right angles" to every other file and thereby cross-references with it, while avoiding interference. Potential information is hidden behind the "icon" of an actual object so that too much is not shown at one time. It is a method of storage and retrieval that animal cells have evolved to deal with large quantities of sensory data, and it has served them well. Plants and single-cell organisms do not need so highly structured a database.

Visual consciousness corresponds to a space dimension as do hearing and smelling, but plays a more important role than either in the overall structure of perceptual consciousness. The space–time of perceptual consciousness *as a whole* is derived from visual perception alone. Light provides an additional realm of consciousness and a corresponding space dimension, but also a structural basis for intercoordinating all five perceptual realms. The photon screen becomes a format for the quantum screen. Touching and tasting, as well as hearing and smelling, are incorporated into the dimensional structure of seeing, creating a single space–time structure and a single world. Hearing and smelling remain intercellular media separate from light, but objects heard and smelled become dimensional patterns based on the structure of light. Light is its own intercellular medium for visual experience, but it is also a *universal intercellular medium* in that the other spatial realms have adopted its structure. This structure is derived from the constant c, where one second equals 186,000 miles. This is why space itself has the structural properties of light.

What I have called the photon screen is visual consciousness only, and the quantum screen, perceptual consciousness as a whole. They are of the same fundamental structure. The photon screen is actual vision and the quantum screen potential vision. The photon screen originates with the sensation of a single photon on a single cell in the retina. What the cell "feels" we "see," as this single bit of information is arranged with many billions of others into a dimensional pattern. It is hard to experience the photon screen as a whole because one tends to be distracted by objects *on* the screen, and because one tries to make the screen itself an object in space–time, which it cannot be. The photon screen cannot be on itself. To experience the photon screen as a whole then, it is necessary to see it the way retinal cells feel it — that is, *not in space*. We are not used to seeing things not in space, and perhaps *seeing* is the wrong word, but it is possible to experience the photon screen as a whole if one does not expect it to be in space and is not distracted by what is happening on it. The quantum screen is also not in space, and must be experienced the same way. It is an extrapolation and extension of the photon screen, extending infinitely in all directions in space, time, and mass. We hear, smell, taste, and touch on the quantum screen. But we also see on it. The photon screen is the visual portion of the much greater quantum screen. The quantum screen is derived from the photon screen, but once established, the photon screen becomes part of it.

Why, you may ask at this point, go to such trouble to explain the fundamental structure of the universe (space–time) within light, and thus within consciousness? Is it not simpler to keep space and time external to consciousness, with light bouncing off material objects? We put space–time within light because that is where physicists have found it. They have defined space in terms of light and they can find nothing *in* space that carries light. Space breaks down where objects are as small as light, or as fast, or as distant or massive as light is able to show them. Light is a particle on the quantum (cellular) level, and a wave on the macroscopic (multicellular) level. Physicists know that space and time are "quantized," and "grainy," and that extremely small objects move discontinuously, like a dot on a computer screen. They know that a photon is a "light quantum" and that space and time get their relation to each other, and to mass, from light. It is convenient to think of light in space only because it is customary. With what we now know, it is simpler to think of space as a structure of intercellular consciousness derived from the structure of light.

As the quantum screen coordinates all perceptual realms with vision, the body becomes a shape in space. The tactile realm jumps onto the quantum screen and takes its place in relation to other objects. Where we see it, or an arm or a leg of it, in space is where we potentially feel it. But where the information potentials of the higher realms become space dimensions, that of tactile consciousness becomes a second time dimension. It would be more convenient to have another space dimension for this purpose, but that is not how the dimensional cards are dealt. Instead, to know an object's location in the second time dimension (mass), we need to put together several time-separated perceptions of its motion through space. To measure its acceleration, we need to "sniff out" the mass dimension the way an olfactory observer sniffs out the second and third space dimensions. We must construct it in time. This "foreshortening" of mass in space–time means that we cannot know an object's mass by looking at it, but must guess it by identifying the object, its size, and possible density. All this, of course, is derived from previous experience.

The tactile realm, as a shape on the quantum screen, and with its corresponding mass dimension, is the pivot of doing. Nothing can be done with the objects that are seen and heard and smelled until they are contacted by the body (directly or indirectly). This is accomplished through interchanging mass with space and time dimensions as we accelerate the whole body, or part of it, to where and when something is perceived. We "scroll" though space as we walk down the hall, or turn our head, or move an arm, and we feel corresponding sensations in the tactile realm. We feel the second time dimension through the parts of the body that are accelerated. But doing requires more than the five perceptual realms and their dimensions. *What* we do is something we have to *think* of and not something on the quantum screen at all. The context of "doable" thought is yet another dimension-like potential that reveals itself as *order* in space–time–mass. (Like mass in 4-D space–time, "order" is foreshortened in 5-D space–time–mass.) It is thoughtful acceleration of the body, or parts of the body, that creates order and survival, and that distinguishes living from inanimate objects.

What we perceive in the higher senses are arrangements of actual chemo-tactile perceptions of our sensory cells within the structure of the quantum screen. Spatial potentials, therefore, originate within intercellular being. With spatial potentials comes choice, and the possibility of doing in space. We may come or go; we may turn this way or that; we may pick up the pen where we see it on the desk or leave it where it is. The self that does the doing is an actual within space. Space is a potential within being.

Self arises among individual cells when they do things together. It is the vantage point from which order is perceived, and the pivot point between the tactile realm (the body) and doable thought. It is what does the doing. It is that which interchanges dimensions in order to rearrange what is perceived. But as soon as something is done, something else is not done, and as soon as there is order, there is disorder, or a competing order from some other perspective. Unlike being, self exists within space and time and mass — an actual within a potential — and because it is only one of many possibilities, the self exists in a fractured and conditional world. It is never fully aware of what is because it is more concerned with what could be, and thus with what is not. The self is a creation of the dimensions, in that it could not exist without the potential being that they provide. Objects appear to the self in space–time surrounded by clouds of thought, uncertainty, and potential manipulation. Self sees even itself in space–time. It understands the body as an object along with other objects and other selves. With self, being is confined within potential being, and there is the creation of things not actual, and therefore of nonbeing. Potentials divide consciousness into subject and object, self and nonself, being and nonbeing. The physical universe that the self is in is so large that nearly all of it is not seen and not touched. I do not see what is happening behind my head, in the next room, or on the outer moons of Jupiter. Actual experience is forced into the infinities of space and time, and the self feels insignificant in relation to the whole. When it begins doing, it must think of what to do, and therefore of what not to do. It becomes aware of all that can never be. This is stressful, and creates the anxiety, and the interest, and the vitality of being an organism.

Self can only glimpse the wholeness of being, and when it does, it cannot do, and is no longer itself. But selves are what we are as organisms, and what we are during the time that we are in.

The wholeness of being is restored by the realization that dimensions are "actual" potential perception. Empty space becomes consciousness, and we experience all that is. Nonbeing becomes being not in time. It is only a glimpse because it is not in time and not in self. The self cannot see the potentials because it is in them.

Being an Organization

A NATION, A CLASS, A NEIGHBORHOOD, OR A BASEBALL TEAM DEVELOPS, TO ONE degree or another, a collective self. Members begin to see things the same way, to interact in a mutually beneficial manner, and to create an institutional order that sustains their wholeness. They become each other and do things as a team. Yet there is space between them.

Consciousness seems to flow through the space between them in the form of information. Information is orderly energy, and of the same dimensional components as orderly behavior. The difference is that behavior requires considerable energy and any degree of order, while information requires little energy and a high degree of order. Stacking a cord of firewood takes a lot of energy and some order, while writing a letter takes very little energy and a lot of order. They are both forms of doing. Consciousness is more likely to "flow" through the latter than the former.

Language, oral or written, has been the most highly developed form of information in human societies. It distinguishes humans from animals more than does anything else. But collective selves are not exclusive to humans or to language among humans. A flock of blackbirds is a collective self, as is a school of fish. Each displays highly ordered collective behavior and constitutes a wholeness more than its parts without what we would call language. Honeybees, termites, and farmer ants are an even greater organic wholeness in that they not only move collectively, but divide labor among themselves in food gathering, defense, and reproduction. The behavior of a bivouac of army ants is virtually indistinguishable from that of a single multicellular organism. The collective behavior of these arthropods is amazing to us because we think of consciousness as within the confines of each separate organism, and wonder how each individual ant or termite "knows" what it is supposed to do. The degree of communication necessary for such highly ordered collective behavior is something we tend to think only the human brain is capable of producing. The higher species of our next closest phylum seem to have evolved collective selves more tightly interwoven, in many cases, than our own through mostly chemotactile forms of communication.

Human language differs from other forms of communication, I believe, in that it is symbolic. I cannot say this for certain because there may be a degree of symbolism in the hoof stomping of an antelope, the growl of a mountain gorilla, or the dance of a honeybee, but I suspect that it is much more highly developed among humans. By symbolism I mean the encoding of actual into potential experience. A symbol is something that means more than it actually is. Symbolic language is more than a "grunt and point"; it is not merely getting your attention to make you look at what I am seeing, but a description of what I am seeing that makes your actual seeing unnecessary. What I say I see is what you *would* see if you were where I am. All you *actually* perceive are sounds coming out of my mouth, but the order in which those sounds are arranged tells you something about the world that you do not actually perceive. What is essential to the structure of human collective consciousness is the relation between what you hear me say and what you see for yourself when you come over to where I am standing. The two have to be dimensionally coordinated. If I say there is a large yellow dog just outside the window I am looking through, and you do not see it, there is no collective consciousness. If you do see it, you may suppose that is because it is "really there," but what you have actually experienced is a dimensional coordination between what you see and what you heard me tell you. It is through this structure of consciousness that humans are able to "see through each other's eyes."

Collective consciousness is the "observational" realm of consciousness. It consists of information from observers, and is always potential perception. It is what would appear in the perceptual realms under the conditions the observer says he is experiencing. It is *reducible* to sounds and shapes, and thus to actual perception, but its orderliness constructs the higher realm of consciousness. The structural relation between individual and collective experience is thus the same as that between single cellular and multicellular experience. The reduction of language to sound is analogous to the reduction of light or sound to tactile perception.

Organizations, or collective selves, are an orderly behavior not only of individuals, but also among individuals. They are experienced in the same realm as individual observers, and differ from them only in that they are an order over and above the order displayed by the individuals themselves. A marching band is an organization because everybody is in step. Each individual in the band moves in an orderly manner in his own right, even when out of step, but the band becomes a collective self only when the individuals within it conform to the order of the band as a whole. Being in step indicates that each individual could tell us something about the world not only from his individual perspective, but also from the perspective of the band as a whole. Each is likely to know the conductor's musical preferences, the rehearsal schedule, and John Sousa's middle name. The strength of the band as an organization can be determined by the conformity of the information each of its members understands. If information flows well, the band will have a strong identity, and will get things done. But if some band members know the rehearsal schedule and others do not, there may be some out of step at the next parade.

When individuals form an organization, they do things that benefit others within the organization as much as they benefit themselves directly. They become, to that extent, what the organization is. But in doing selflessly for an organization they do not transcend self, they merely form another, larger self. The collective self may be as selfish as an individual self, or more so. Organizations have selves because we want them to do things. We want school boards to teach children, businesses to provide goods and services, and governments to defend against other governments. Every organization has to develop its own experience, its own point of view, and its own sense of identity. Like an individual self, the collective self must have an ego that tells itself who it is in relation to others, and what it can do in relation to what it has already done. The self of an organization is the same as that of an organism, except it exists only in the observational realm of consciousness and not the perceptual realms. It does not see or hear or touch, nor is it seen or heard or touched. Parts of the whole may be seen and heard and touched, but the organization itself is not. We may see a boardroom, a busy office, or an army marching off to battle, but we cannot see an organization. We see only the order that it manifests in space and time and mass.

But at what point does an organization become a being? There is no answer to this question because "*a*" being implies that there are other beings, and that being is divided. Being is not *in* an organization any more than it is in an organism or a cell. An organization does not *have* being or consciousness. Consciousness is what is *experienced*; it is not in a self, collective or otherwise. You or I experience "being an organization" if we exchange information with one another and with other observers. If, on the other hand, we do not exchange information but merely perceive the orderly behavior of a group, we experience the observational potential without experiencing its actualization. We experience the organization either way, but we experience *being* the organization only when we know what it knows and do what it does. Only when the organization tells us something about the world that we do not experience directly do we experience actual observational consciousness.

Oral language limits organizational being to the present. I hear what you are saying now, but as soon as you say it, it is gone. I will forget it tomorrow, and so will you. That is why you should write it down. As soon as you write it on a piece of paper, or a clay tablet, it transcends time and space. You can take it with you wherever you go, send it to your partner in a distant city, or show it to me tomorrow, or next year, or drop it on the ground and let somebody else dig it up four thousand years from now. We will still know what you said. Your words will still be alive and observational consciousness will flow through them.

Writing is of the same dimensional components as oral language, but vastly expands the range and the intensity of human organizations by encoding thought and experience in a "material" form — that is, in a form that is potentially perceivable at other times and places. It has made cities and empires and distant ventures possible. It has spread human organizations over vast expanses of Earth and history, and greatly strengthened their power in relation to nature and to each other. Without writing there would be no streets and no bridges, no schools and no factories, no orchestras and no museums. There would be no history. The civilization that we now know is the creation of written language.

But where writing has created strength within human organizations, it has fractured humanity itself. There is no one system of writing that everyone may understand, and therefore no human organization that we may all be. An ideographic or pictographic writing system, such as Chinese calligraphy or Egyptian hieroglyphics, might have become a universal medium by avoiding connections to oral language, but phonetic systems have proven more wieldy. Phonetic systems are easier to learn because they parallel oral language. You don't have to learn a whole new set of words and ideas to learn to write. But they are more limiting for the same reason. You remain confined by the self of your oral tradition when you learn to write. Phonetic writing systems have led to the evolution of separate national literary traditions, and indirectly to the formation of separate national sovereignties. Instead of a human tradition, we have many separate national traditions, each reading its own books and newspapers and developing its own versions of history. We feel that we are Russian or Korean or German first and human second. We have learned how to do what is best for our countries, but we do not know how to do what is best for humanity.

THIS HAS NOT BEEN A GREAT PROBLEM UNTIL RECENTLY. SEPARATE EMPIRES AND nations have done what they have needed to do and humanity has been fruitful and multiplied. But now we have great oceans to tend, and an atmosphere to care for. We did not have to care for them before. Deforestation in Indonesia affects temperatures in North Africa and hurricanes in the Caribbean. Refrigerants in the United States and Europe cause skin cancer in China. Over-population in Mexico spills into California and Texas. Separate governments do little because they are parts and not the whole. The earth must be tended as a whole, and we must now tend it. But we are not now who we need to be to do it. Doing cannot be done until being has become.

Becoming happens through awareness, through looking at what is. You cannot push it or tug it. You cannot make it happen, but you have to be there when it does happen. You have to see it. It begins as a flame at the edge of the fireball, becomes an image and a thought, and finally a thing and a truth known to all. It begins as a toy, becomes a tool, and then an organ. Looking into artificial space on a cathode ray tube is looking into who we are becoming. This is the new screen. Language is no longer the primary vehicle of collective consciousness.

Electronic images do not do anything, and will not save us, but they are what we will be.

Chapter 9

The Perceptual Solipsism

WESTERN PHYSICS, WITHIN WESTERN METAPHYSICS, POINTS TO SOLIPSISM. WE HAVE found that the observer is integral to what is observed. What I see depends on me seeing it and is, therefore, me. If consciousness is the ultimate reality, and it is mine, everything is me. The world is me. This is the full logic of what we now know.

It should be rejected because it is complicated and repugnant. Complicated because I cannot without difficulty explain the apparent consciousness of others as an aspect of my own, and repugnant because I do not want to be alone and full of myself. Solipsism, however, remains logical. The closer one looks at an independently existing world, the less one sees. If there is nothing more logical, and principles of science are to be followed, solipsism should be accepted, no matter how ugly it may be. This will not be the first time a worldview repulsive to fundamental moral sensitivities has had to be accepted in the name of science.

But the solipsism is rejected ultimately not because of its ugliness, but because of its complexity. It is too hard to find explanations for why you do what you do, if you are really part of me. The problem is not consciousness; the problem is me. Why does consciousness have to be me? If it is inside of my skull it has to be me, but if my skull is inside it, it does not. If space and time are a structure of consciousness, and "matter" is an actualization within the structure, consciousness is not in my skull or in me. There is no identity between self and consciousness.

Self is the perspective of *perceptual* consciousness. We see, hear, feel, etc. from the standpoint of self. The apparent identity of self and consciousness arises from this role. But the same self is not the standpoint of *observational* consciousness. Observational consciousness is a wholeness over and above the separate selves that create and sustain it. It is an order that transcends its particulars, and a reality more fundamental than its contents. Observational *information* is experienced from the standpoint of individual self because it is reduced to the sights and sounds that are perceived by self. But it is only in its reduced form that it is experienced from the standpoint of self. Observational consciousness remains independent of any individual self: yours, mine, or anybody else's.

If observational consciousness is safely understood in this manner, *perceptual* consciousness may be understood as a solipsism. We may comfortably allow for the existence of only one perceptual consciousness if assured that it is not the whole of consciousness. What "I see," "I hear," etc. is perceptual; what "he hears" or "she sees" or "you touch" is not. If there is only one perceptual consciousness, there are also realms of conscious reality that are not perceptual. Himself or yourself remains a perspective of observational information (a point in space–time from which "I" *would* see what he or she says they are seeing) and a locus of order, but not a separate perceptual consciousness. He and she do things that create order and that keep them alive, but they only appear "conscious." There is a distinct structural difference, and a distinct *physical* difference, therefore, between "my" self and all other selves. All selves are focal points of doing, but only "my" self includes perceptual consciousness. In the observational realm all selves are equivalent, including "my" self. As soon as I say what I see and feel, and listen to what you say you see and feel, yourself and myself become morally, and physically, equivalent.

Observational consciousness exists only by the moral and physical equivalence of individual selves. It is by definition potential perceptual consciousness; what I say I see must be what you or anyone else would say they see from the same perspective. In the perceptual realms, "you" are "no more than" an orderly arrangement of symbols indicating potential perception. But being is not limited to perceptual consciousness. With the moral equivalence of selves, being is no longer rooted in what "I" see or feel. Being becomes rooted in what I *potentially* see or feel, as communicated by you. Potential perception becomes as real as actual; I feel your pain without perceiving it directly. Your pain is as real as my own, though I do not experience it in a perceptual realm. "Your" perceptual experience is not actualized for me, only what you say you feel. "I" do not become "you," but "we" become a being greater than both of us separately.

RELIGION AND MORALITY TEACH THAT YOUR EXPERIENCE IS AS REAL AS MINE. THIS is a great truth that there is no way to perceive. It is known only through being.

There is tension in life between self and others, between actual and potential perception. It is tension not between one consciousness and another, but between one level and another of the same consciousness. This distinction is fundamental to understanding what we now know of the world. The balance is tipping away from actual toward potential perception with advances in communications technology. We are becoming a higher level of being. We know more of the world through the eyes of others.

RELIGION IS CONSCIOUSNESS BEYOND SELF.

THE CUP YOU SEE ON THE COUNTER IS REALLY THERE IN THE SENSE THAT YOU WILL really touch it if you reach out to the space and time that it occupies. The truck you see speeding down the highway is really there in that it will hurt you if you do not avoid its path. Potential perception is as real as actual, even *within* the perceptual realms. Most of experience is potential perception. Most of what we do is in reaction to potential, and not actual, experience. We keep our fingers from the flame because we see it burning, not because we feel it burning. We step around snakes not because they are biting us, but because we do not wish to be bitten. We limit and control actual experiences through complex dimensional interchanges that actualize desirable perceptions. This keeps us alive.

Think of the things you do to make a living. You put on a clean shirt, walk around the corner to the train station, sit at your desk and punch little buttons. There is no actual money in any of these, no actual experience of the things you want to experience, but you have to do it to be paid. The money is not actual food or fun or shelter, only a means to food or shelter. You have to go buy food and cook it before you eat. And you pay the heating bill *before* you are cold. You react to potential rather than actual experience.

Other living beings, though we do not experience their actual perceptions, are as real and alive as are we ourselves. When I say that there is a solipsism of perceptual consciousness I do not mean that other people or animals are not alive or have no feelings. Quite the contrary: Every observer is a world as real as what we perceive directly. Every ant, every amoeba, every cell in the blade of grass under your foot is an entire world of sensation and feeling. Every friend and loved one and every old lady you help across the street is a universe of stars and galaxies equal to what you see with your own eyes. It is not actual only in that their experience is unavailable in the perceptual realms. Language creates the reality, if not the actuality, of this experience, and makes actualization unnecessary. We do not have to go where they are to see for ourselves what they are seeing. When we live with and love other people, potential perception is as real as direct perception. This is all the law and the prophets.

SO WHAT DIFFERENCE DOES THE PERCEPTUAL SOLIPSISM MAKE? NONE, REALLY. WE are looking at what is and it looks the same. You will never directly see what I see no matter what we call it. The difference is the understanding of what is seen and what is said. There is a new label on a new filing system. That is the only difference.

Christmas in the Trenches

My name is Francis Tolliver, I come from Liverpool,
Two years ago the war was waiting for me after school.
To Belgium and to Flanders, to Germany to here,
I fought for King and country I love dear.

'Twas Christmas in the trenches, where the frost so bitter hung,
The frozen fields of France were still, no Christmas song was sung.
Our families back in England were toasting us that day,
Their brave and glorious lads so far away.

I was lying with my messmate on the cold and rocky ground,
When across the lines of battle came a most peculiar sound.
Says I, "Now listen up, me boys!" Each soldier strained to hear,
As one young German voice sang out so clear.

"He's singing bloody well, you know!" my partner says to me,
Soon one by one each German voice joined in harmony.
The cannons rested silent, the gas clouds rolled no more,
As Christmas brought us respite from the war.

As soon as they were finished and a reverent pause was spent,
"God Rest Ye Merry, Gentlemen" struck up some lads from Kent.
The next they sang was "Stille Nacht." "Tis 'Silent Night'," says I,
And in two tongues one song filled up that sky.

"There's someone coming toward us!" the front line sentry cried,
All sights were fixed on one lone figure trudging from their side.
His truce flag, like a Christmas star, shown on that plain so bright,
As he, bravely, strode unarmed into the night.

Soon one by one on either side walked into No Man's Land,
With neither gun nor bayonet we met there hand to hand.
We shared some secret brandy and we wished each other well,
And in a flare-lit soccer game we gave 'em hell.

We traded chocolates, cigarettes, and photographs from home,
These sons and fathers far away from families of their own.
Young Sanders played his squeezebox and they had a violin,
This curious and unlikely band of men.

Soon daylight stole upon us and France was France once more,
With sad farewells we each prepared to settle back to war.
But the question haunted every heart that lived that wondrous night,
"Whose family have I fixed within my sights?"

Twas Christmas in the trenches where the frost, so bitter hung,
The frozen fields of France were warmed as songs of peace were sung.
For the walls they'd kept between us to exact the work of war,
Had been crumbled and were gone forevermore.

My name is Francis Tolliver, in Liverpool I dwell,
Each Christmas come since World War I, I've learned its lessons well.
That the ones who call the shots won't be among the dead and lame,
And on each end of the rifle we're the same.[4]

A Day in the Box

THERE IS A VERY SMALL CHURCH IN A TOWN I USED TO LIVE IN, AND AS I WALK INSIDE
with my wife, there is a man I know kneeling with two or three other people.
They see us and rise, but we do not join them. Instead, we walk through a
hallway off to one side and there is a small cabinet door, which is already
open. Inside there is a woman I do not know, who steps out and excuses her-
self as she passes by. I do not know if I am supposed to go in. My wife, I think,
is still with me, and that is all I remember.

The sun is already shining through my window, and I am glad that I do
not have to be anywhere early today. The coffee is already made, and I can
smell it in the kitchen. Somebody is opening and closing cupboards. I think
of getting dressed and moving in that direction, but there is no hurry. I turn
over and feel the mattress pushing softly on my hip and shoulder. I am thankful for a warm bed, and a roof, and what looks like a beautiful day, but my
mind wanders to a phone call I must make before going out, and to the drain
under the bathroom sink. The trap and stopper assembly has become corroded
and is leaking where they join. Loft's, I think, has a kit that I could install, but
Hunsinger's would be more on my way if I have to drop off the declarations
page at the insurance agent. I will call there before I decide. Hunsinger's is
likely to be cheaper, too…. There is another curve in the… but no…

I hear traffic and it reminds me to be in it, and I turn back over and push
the pillow over to the other side of the bed. I feel my right ear between my
shoulder and the weight of my head. The child in the movie last night was
attractive, but not convincing as an actor. I give it a B–, but I am thinking of
it the next day, which, I remind myself, is one of my definitions of a good
movie. This will not last, though, and I swing my feet around and sit up on

the edge of the bed, watching them touch the floor. Gravity flows from my hips as I stand and look through the blinds to the street. There is no one there yet, but I hear a neighbor in the next yard saying something as he closes his car door. He has already had coffee, I think.

Later I am driving down West Churchill Street, wondering if the light at Purdue will be green when I get there. If it is, I will go straight, but it will be a long wait if not, and I would do better to get in the right lane now in case I decide to make a quick right turn and stop at the post office before heading up Limestone to Hunsinger's. But there is a truck in the right lane ahead of me. He shifts gears up the hill and lets out a small puff of smoke. Diesel. Must have a load. I don't want to be behind him, but he is accelerating and I am not sure if I can get ahead before Purdue.

The guy ahead of me isn't in any hurry, either. No rush. I relax a little, but gain on the truck. I hear a plane passing overhead and think of two hundred and thirty passengers sitting with their folding tables in the upright position listening to music through wires in their ears, and of trillions of air molecules rushing over and under the wings. A few more pass under than over, and this creates a partial vacuum that lifts the plane enough to keep it in the air. But so much weight! Just that little difference in pressure, just those few extra molecules bumping on the bottom of the wing....

The truck shifts gears again, and I think of being on the surface of this planet, of the pavement and the earth under the pavement, holding me, and the truck, against gravity. But why should we be held? A strange substance, this gravity. Always there, pulling on things without explanation. We never think of it. I feel it in the car seat beneath me as I catch up with the truck in the right lane. But why think of gravity at all? It is just there, pulling on things, whether I am thinking of it or not. What more can be thought, and to what avail? The truck slows and I will not have space to pass it. The light is red. I come to an easy stop, feeling a slight pressure on the seat belt. Truck brakes squeal and jerk.

Up past the plane the air molecules thin, and there is no use for wings. Gravity must be countered with more brutal forces before it, too, begins to thin. There is a point somewhere between the earth and moon, where the gravity of each is exactly counterbalanced by the other, and you could just sit there without falling toward either. There must be other such points between Earth and the sun, and the other planets and other suns. But with a relative velocity you don't need them; at the right distance you could orbit without falling anyway. But what would space really be in that situation? What would it feel like? Is it just something you move through in any direction without bumping into things. If it is just emptiness, is it anything at all? Am I really anywhere if there is nothing else around?

I remember that space is only relative; it only exists as defined by the things that are in it. But what if nothing is in it? Out past the last galaxies is it still there? There can be no end because the end would have to be in something. I remember thinking as a kid that there must be a wall of some kind at the very end of space, and "nothing" on the other side. But the light is green now and I see a puff of smoke from the truck. I will stop at the post office on my way back. It will mean left turns coming and going, but I am in no hurry. Life is better when there is no hurry, even with left turns.

The truck lunges forward as the engine roars. Gears grind with another shift, but I am already ahead of him, and shove the turn signal down. It is another two blocks, but the right lane is clear ahead, and I will position myself well in advance this time. I remember seeing EASTERN FREIGHT SERVICES written on the trailer. I wonder what he is hauling. The road is level now, but he is still straining under the load. I picture boxes inside, crates maybe, with metal straps holding them together on wooden pallets. Inside the boxes are parts — probably gears or something — but definitely made of steel, with rows of carriage bolts across each side. There is ninetyweight gear oil within each casing and celluloid gaskets between the metal parts. Gear oil sloshes backward as the truck accelerates and then forward again as he shifts into high range.

I ease into the right lane ahead of the truck and watch it recede in my rearview mirror, thinking of all the protons and neutrons in quadrillions of crated iron atoms holding the truck back behind me. How do they do it? What are they pulling against? I think of the earth pulling them down against each other and against the wooden pallets, bending the suspension of the trailer and squeezing the tires against the pavement. The pavement again. But the question here is one of forward motion. Even if there were no gravity, if the boxes of gear housings were in a rocket ship in interstellar space, all those subatomic particles would be holding back against space itself, keeping the ship from accelerating as fast I can in my lighter ship. But if space is relative, what do the protons and neutrons have their claws in? There must be something in, or "of," space that is independent of gravity and independent of the objects that are in space. But I have heard that this is wrong.

I will, however, reach the corner far ahead of the truck and make my right turn on a green light. With luck I will pick up the drain parts and be back home well before lunch, after a quick stop at the post office. I might even get a start on the repair work itself before stopping to eat — open the package and read the directions, things like that. I like to get a scope on a job and think about it a little anyway. Okay, here's Hunsinger's. Hope they have the right one. But I hate that speed bump in the parking lot. The guy ahead of me tries to go around it to the right, but his left tire hits it anyway. I see it coming toward me (or me toward it) and anticipate the jolt as my tires bump up and over. It's there for a purpose, I know, but I hate it.

Inside, the aisle clerk is patient. He is known as an "associate" now. He helps me find the stopper assembly but I have forgotten the size. Either an inch and a quarter or an inch and a half. I should have brought the old one, but I had it in my hand an hour ago, and the inch and a quarter feels closer to it. I hold it between my thumb and index finger and look at its shiny surface. Electroplated chromium probably. This little item was in an electrolyte bath just last week, somewhere in Wisconsin. Maybe this is what was in the back of the truck....

In the parking lot there is a man leaving on a bicycle. He is wearing a helmet with a rearview mirror attached. On the way to the post office I feel the day getting warmer, and I open the sunroof to let out some heat. On the way home I will close everything up and switch on the air conditioning. I pass a bus full of people. A woman drives by the other way talking on a cell phone.

Realm Number Five or Is It Two

WHY DO WE FEEL THAT BEING IS INSIDE THE BODY?

LET US SAY THAT YOU ARE IN A LARGE ROOM SOMEWHERE IN INTERSTELLAR SPACE. There is no gravity and you are at rest in relation to the walls of the room. You see your arms and legs in front of you and see other objects floating about the room, but so far you have not come into contact with any of them. You can move parts of the body, but not the body as a whole. No matter how much you wiggle and squirm, you can get no closer to or farther from any of the walls or objects you see around you. You feel your arms and legs moving, but because you cannot push off anything or grab hold of anything, you feel no overall acceleration. You can't go anywhere and are at rest in space–time, and also in space–time–time.

Now let us say you see a football heading your way and it hits you. For simplicity, let us say that you do not reach out to catch it or move any part of your body in relation to it; it just hits you head-on and bounces off. As it comes into contact, you see that your whole body begins to move slightly toward one of the walls of the room and you feel a g force throughout the body. While the football is pushing you, you are not at rest in space–time or space–time–time. You are accelerating. But as it bounces off, you stop accelerating, your velocity stabilizes, and you no longer feel the g force. You have come to rest in space–time–time, but you are no longer at rest in space–time because you keep moving at a constant speed relative to the walls of the room. You feel space–time–time (the mass dimension) while under acceleration, but you do not feel space–time while under constant velocity.

You have experienced the body in two separate realms — the tactile and the visual. The body felt is the tactile realm itself, or actual tactile perception as a whole, while the body seen is potential tactile perception. (The hand that you see out in front of you is where and when you will touch, not actual touch.) You *felt* the g force only while in actual tactile contact with the football, but you *see* that it has changed your potential tactile relation to the walls of the room and to all the objects in the room. The body felt is not *in* space–time; it does not feel space. It does not feel space passing through it nor does it feel itself passing through space. Without the visual realm you would have had no idea that you were in the room or that there were objects floating by you. All you would know is that you felt a g force when something the shape of a football contacted you. But you would not think of the g force as "acceleration" or any form of motion, only as an overall tactile sensation. You would not know that you had moved in space or that there was such a thing as space.

The body felt, or actual tactile perception, corresponds to the mass dimension, which is at "right angles" to space–time but not *in* space–time any more than one space dimension is in another. This is the same thing as the second time dimension. But without vision it would not be coordinated with space at all. Without vision you would have no sense of accelerating in relation to the walls of the room or anything else, and there would be no use for a second time dimension. It is only to coordinate the visual with the tactile realm that mass becomes a dimension at "right angles" to space–time. It is only to coordinate what we see with what we feel that the body seen becomes a location for the body felt. The body seen is always in space–time; there is no other way to perceive it. But the body felt is not inherently spatial; space is superimposed upon it. You do not need space to feel touch.

THE BODY SEEN IS IN SPACE. THE BODY FELT IS NOT. BUT THEY ARE THE SAME THING.

YOU NEED THE BODY IN SPACE TO KEEP THINGS TIDY. YOU "FILE" ACTUAL TACTILE perceptions within the space outlined by the body seen just to keep things tidy. This makes it seem as though part of being ("your" part) is "inside" the body. It makes it seem as though things you actually feel take place inside the space the body seen occupies. It is perhaps because the body seen is so close in space that you think of "your being" as within it. But it may be only because you are being too tidy that you put being anywhere. Or call it yours.

THE TACTILE REALM, THE SECOND REALM (AFTER THE CHEMICAL), CORRESPONDS to the mass dimension, which comes after time (the fourth dimension, historically speaking) — a fifth dimension, or a second. They are all interchangeable, anyway.

But what about the objects you see floating about in the room? They are not in or on the body and you do not feel them. They are not in the tactile realm. In what sense, then, are they in the mass dimension?

If you only see them, they are only potentially tactile. Their location in mass (their behavior in the second time dimension) tells you the magnitude of the acceleration your body will feel if and when you make contact. If the football is full of lead instead of air you will feel a greater magnitude. But you cannot tell the football's mass just by looking at it. You have to watch it interact with other objects. It will change its velocity drastically when colliding with more massive objects and move only slightly when colliding with less massive ones. You can determine its mass only after repeated perceptions of its behavior in space–time. As you watch the football bouncing off tables and chairs and toothpicks and boulders you realize that each object has a location on an invisible scale from "light" to "heavy," and that this location is directly proportional to what it feels like when you collide with it. If there were another space dimension, and it corresponded to mass, you could see each object's location on the scale immediately, but because space is superimposed on mass (or mass on space) you cannot even tell that there is a mass dimension at any one time. You need several times. Five-dimensional space–time–time is foreshortened into four-dimensional space–time and only shows up as you watch an object's behavior over time.

Now let us say, for the sake of complexity, that we subject your interstellar room to an accelerating force. Suddenly, the whole room begins to move faster and faster in one direction. One of the walls moves toward you at an ever-increasing speed, while the opposite wall moves away. You do not feel anything different at first, and you see all the objects in the room right where they were in relation to each other and to you. Only the walls of the room are moving. But one by one the tables and chairs and boulders and footballs, and you, collide with the approaching wall. There is now a sort of "floor" to your room even though it is no different from any of the other walls. It is fairly smooth, but not perfectly so, and you feel it constantly pushing against your body as it goes faster and faster through space, taking you with it. After the floor has caught up with all the objects in the room you "stand up" and look around. A chair that had floated up to you only minutes before now lies against the wall that is now the floor. You pick it "up" off the floor and throw it away from you. The floor comes crashing up to it; it slides for a short distance across the floor, and then comes to a stop. Always before when you pushed it away (before the floor started accelerating), it kept going in a straight line at a constant speed without interacting with anything until it bounced off one of the walls and came back toward you.

So what is happening? The accelerating force that you are experiencing has changed the relation of the room to every object in the room. They are no longer isolated from each other, and their identities are no longer entirely separate. Their masses are now interrelated, and you cannot see the full measure of each individual object's behavior in the second time dimension. They all share the same location in that dimension to some extent. The chair came to a stop because it is now in relation with the floor. You may not have noticed, but as the chair came to a stop, the whole room accelerated slightly in the direction of its motion. This counterbalanced an acceleration of the whole room in the opposite direction that you produced as you threw the chair away from you with your feet against the floor. The chair, the floor, you, and all the footballs and toothpicks lying on the floor are all related by friction. All are now at one with the floor *in the mass dimension*. This is a dimensional interchange, or a rotation of the axes of space–time–mass into the mass dimension.

But what has caused it? A large rocket engine attached to the outside of the room that somebody suddenly fired up? You have no way of knowing because you have never seen outside the room. You suppose that if there were a window that you could look through, you would see everything outside zooming past at faster and faster speeds. The g force you have felt in your body ever since the floor collided with you tells you that the room remains under constant acceleration, and this means greater and greater velocity in relation to everything that is not accelerating. But suppose you look around and *do* find a window that you had not noticed before, and you look through it. Instead of seeing everything zooming past as you expected, you see houses and trees that are not moving at all. They are at rest in relation to you and the room. They, too, must be accelerating at the same constant rate. But in relation to what? Then you realize what has happened. Your room, rather than being "at rest" in interstellar space, was falling through a gravitational field all along, until it collided with the surface of the gravitating body. Luckily, it was a planet small enough and with weak enough gravity to cause minimum damage upon impact. But now everything in your room, and everything you do, will be in relation to it. You and everything around you, are at one in the mass dimension with this little planet.

THROUGH GRAVITY WE ARE ALL RELATED TO THE EARTH. SEPARATE IN SPACE, WE are all one thing: plants, animals, rocks, air. The soil pushes up, accelerating to a standstill, gathering. The body comes up through the feet.

I THINK OF BEING IN MY BODY ALSO BECAUSE, OF ALL THE PERCEPTUAL REALMS, the only one in which I can do anything is the tactile. I need my body to push things around. Time "passes on" whether I care or not, and space just sits there. But I can make my body do things. I can think of something and then do it by moving arms and legs. The mass dimension is the only one over which I have any control, and it is from within the body that control seems to originate. Thought originates in being and becomes order, as it becomes manifest in dimensions.

But not all thought is doable, and not all doable thought done. Doable thought is a range of consciousness close to the tactile realm, restricted by the dimensions in which it unfolds. It is infinitely smaller than thought itself, and infinitely larger than that actually done. It is anything I *can do*, and therefore a cross section of what I can think of, but an infinite multiple of what I *do* do.

Doable thought is so close to the tactile realm that it is not entirely distinguishable from it. What I do is largely what I want to do, which is to keep my body alive and well. I think of drinking water when I am thirsty, and of moving my arm when it has lain too long in one position. I think of catching the train so that I may get to work on time and feed my family and myself. I think of looking both ways before I cross the street. The order I create in the world as I do things is a projection of my body thinking. It is not only the tactile realm; it is also the chemical realm. Much of what I "feel" as hunger, thirst, well-being, and depression is chemical in origin, as well as much of what I feel kinesthetically and emotionally.

Within the body, or the self, it is impossible to draw discreet lines between thought and chemical and tactile perception. They are closely connected with doing, and with each other, and only distinct as they become manifest "externally," in the dimensions. They are not separate until they are made to be separate. The difference between thought and tactile perception is the difference between what only I experience and what somebody else would (potentially) experience in my place: Only I would be thinking of getting up to walk the dog just now, but anybody else would (probably) feel the hard surface of this chair against my lower back. The sensation in my lower back is perceptual and not conceptual only to the extent that it is perceivable in other realms (and observational to the extent perceivable by other people). But because it is in my body, I cannot see or hear it, and neither could anybody else. It is too close. It is not truly separable from thought, then, and only made so by imposing an external structure of consciousness. The structure that divides perception into realms and constructs the dimensional universe does not divide or construct being. What I feel and touch and think and hunger for are more fundamental than space and time and mass. They are not separate until they become separate in the world.

When I do something, however, I step into the dimensions. I make a choice based on potential perception: I look around at what I see, and think of what I could see. If I walk right I will catch the train to work, if left I will get something to eat, and if straight ahead I will be hit by a truck. I can only do one of these; the other two will never exist physically. The togetherness of thought and body and feeling that is more fundamental than space or time becomes the self that does the doing in space and time. The self is not the seeing or touching or hearing or thinking; it is merely the perspective in space and time and mass from which objects are seen or heard or thought of, and the axis about which dimensions are rotated to get things done. If I decide to turn left, I will feel my body turning left and accelerating along the sidewalk as I see the lamppost scrolling past in the opposite direction. The self is the pivot point between doable thought and the perceptual realms. It is where the dimensions are coordinated.

The self brings being into the world through doing. The order that you and I create as we go about our daily lives is what makes us look "conscious" to each other. Each self is a locus of order. But when being is forced into dimensions, it is fragmented into categories and choices and thoughts of things not done. Things the self decides not to do become nonbeing, and it is non-being that creates anxiety and uncertainty. What if I had turned right? What if I had said something sooner? What if the car won't start? If there were no possibilities, there would be no self. Being in space creates nonbeing in most of space and most of time. Most of the world is emptiness, and most of what is full is never seen or heard. There is nobody looking at all the places on the planets or the stars in the galaxies that stretch for hundreds of millions of years and light-years. There is nobody there to touch them. There is nobody to wonder at the shapes of clouds passing overhead, even here on Earth. Being is so small and meaningless in space that we must despair of our significance. We take up so little room, and do so little: What would the universe know if we were not?

But the self that becomes being in dimensions exists only within them. Before or beneath or outside or beyond them there is no self and nothing that is not. Without potentials there are no choices and nothing not done, and nothing not seen. There is nothing that is not actually perceived or thought. But this place of no self and no nonbeing is not a place. You cannot go to it, for you would be you. It is the nonplace where you are not you watching thoughts become objects and patterns of thinking become space and time. It is there when it is not you looking, and when time is not. It is there when the self dies in time, and does no more.

At the nontime at the extreme of space, where the rhythm of light is so stretched and drawn as to blur the identity of any thing, there is another nonplace that we are beginning to know. It is the same place: the one thing that is every thing and nothing in particular, a singularity. We can just now make it out, looking back in time with the latest telescopes and antennas, burgeoning at the speed of light, pulsing, spewing space, breaking into images and shadows of things. But we will never see it; it is infinitely small and surrounds us. It is we trying to be in it. Its mass is so great as to curve space and time back upon itself and become darkness. But that is why the debris is visible, even now, after all these years.

A Day on the Screen

THE STRAP IS ON MY FACE AGAIN. I PUSH DOWN FROM THE WALL GENTLY, BUT I AM awake now, and might as well stay awake. A door closes in the hallway outside, and I hear muffled voices next door. The sonic barrier is down again, but I don't mind. It is not so bad hearing people around me. If it is also down in the office there will be no work again, which I don't mind either. I have taken to sitting alone on the soldeck, and could bring some work there. Might do that anyway, even if the barrier is all right. The system there is newer than here in the sleeping area, and more dependable. Some things in this section are downright primitive, especially the straps. I remove the harness, move over to the closet, and get dressed. I will bathe later in the weight room.

I rub my eyes and glance around the room. The mag unit and headgear are on the back of the door where I left them, and my briefcase is stuck on the table, but I do not see the F80 pod report that I am supposed to be reading. I did not enclose it, and it could be anywhere. It is not against a wall, or in any obvious place, so I turn the dial next to the door and give the room a few webers. The report is magged, and ought to show up if it is not caught on something. My mag unit on the door pulls against the strap and sinks slowly to the floor. A book, some pens, and a few other pieces of extraneous magged junk drift toward the floor, including the F80 report, which was behind the berth.

I gather the trash and stuff it in a plastic bag attached to the table, and stick the report to the side of my briefcase. Switching the dial back to zero, I grab a strap of the mag unit, unshackle it, and put it on. The new ones are full body, but I like this one better, probably because I am used to it. The panels go only from shoulder to rump. I give the room a weber or two again, and adjust the panels. I unshackle my headgear from the back of the door and put it on. There are already some messages. I always put it on before opening the door because there is still a lot of unmagged stuff in the hallway, and some people have gotten hurt. They ought to mag everything, but pieces always seem to break off and get away. They need to gravitate the whole area before someone gets hurt again. The place could use it anyway. I turn the webers and the lights off, and open the door.

Someone is down at the far end, but the hall is otherwise empty. It must be earlier than I thought, which I like. It is good to be off the clock as much as possible, and I like not knowing the time. I get enough done, I assure myself, that I don't have to think about putting in hours. I know I could do more, but nobody is complaining, and there are other things besides work.

The mag unit is set to GRAVITY, which I turn off, and set it on MANUAL TRANS-PORT. I like to drive, if it is not too crowded. I turn right, and feel the panels tugging gently on the shoulder straps. Somebody passes the other way, on AUTO, reading. She does not look up. Facing up the hallway, I scroll up to MEDIUM. I feel the panels push on my back and then relax. Doors move swiftly past on both sides. I come to an intersection but there is no traffic, and I am swept through without elevating. I pass some people I know talking in a room off to the side and wave. My first contact of the day. There is some slower traffic to the right ahead, and I feel the AUTO kicking in, shoving me gently to the left. I swerve a little further to the left and scroll up to HIGH, just for fun. The panels press my back and shoulders, then release. I switch back to MEDIUM as I see someone ahead that I do not want to pass. I don't like to leave it on HIGH. At the next intersection there is some traffic and I elevate and scroll left, the mag straps pulling hard as I round the corner, and I settle in with the traffic. Everybody is on AUTO, reading, listening to something, or just staring off into space. I don't know anybody, and set it on HIGH again, swerving left where there is little traffic. I swerve back and forth in my lane, to find its limits, and think about the large empty area in the middle of the hall where the mag fields interfere. People are passing by in their headgear and I do not recognize anyone. A call is coming in, so I drop back to MEDIUM and set it to AUTO.

There are more people in the office than I expected. The sonic barriers are up, and the floor is bright with light and activity. Most of the vesper shift has not yet left. I greet two that I used to work with, but they are anxious to finish whatever it is they are doing, and do not stop to talk. As I reach my work space a scrap of unmagged printer tape is floating out of my cube, and I wonder if anyone has been in there. It passes up and over my head as I swing through the doorway, and I reach up and grab it with my other hand. It feels coarse and fibrous between my fingers — not the kind of paper I use — and I wonder where it came from. Besides leaving a mess, I don't like the feeling of anyone else being here, even if they have the right. But the monitor recognizes me and switches on as I strap in, and assures me that no one else has logged in. It is good to feel special.

With the door closed, I remove the headset but leave the mag unit on. Most people take it off while working, but I like its feel better than chair straps, and have found that with just a little weber I don't feel the straps at all. The new units, I have read, use full-body mag units all the time, and no straps at all. That would be extremely comfortable, I know, and it scares me to think of it. I am proud of the legs I still have, but so many people don't care at all anymore, as if the possibility of a full .5 g were so remote that it is not worth staying in shape. I like to get to .35 or .4 every day, and to .5 every once in a while, and I think it is important to be able to function at up to .5 in case it happens again. There is a good chance there will be a general .35 for up to six weeks if we relocate, and I'm afraid some people are going to be miserable. Without full-body packs they'll be complaining nonstop. I know it will bother me a little, especially at night, but I look forward to it. I like walking — everything takes on a new relation to everything else, as if the whole universe were on a new slant. And if the grounds people are not too bent out by it, maybe they'll get this place cleaned up. Mag solutions will never do what a little soap and water can do.

The main screen is still showing an isometric of the pod compartment that we are considering as a replacement for F80 green room irrigator. I will let the circulation tea work on it before I begin to think about its capacity — or overcapacity I should say — for small grain production. They've probably overdone it, and they probably don't want to hear about it, but somebody has to say it, namely me. But I'm not going to think about it yet. I pull up a chart with flow rates plotted against manifold diameters. Nothing conclusive here, but I will have to look at it more closely when we know more about how much circulation is needed, and if the pressure will be significantly affected by the g environment, which will vary. I erase the chart and switch to a live filter of the sol from the soldeck. It never changes much, but I like to look at it every day, just for a minute or two. It is mostly clear, with a small rotating disturbance at about 30 North latitude, just now appearing over the horizon, the same one I saw yesterday. But my message screen pops up over it. Must be the same ones on my headset this morning, but they were all 3 or less urgency. The chart pops up again, and I switch to audio and listen as I reach down and plug the IV to my leg port. This might take a little longer than I thought, and I'm hungry. I was going to eat something real in the weight room today, but my friend George has something else in mind.

By midmorning I have gotten him through his latest anxiety seizure, and I am up and away again. I will have to keep my headset on in case he calls again, and that will keep me away from the weight room until afternoon. Some people work out with the set on, but it is not the same for me. The weight room is the only safe public space to be without a headset, and I find it very liberating to see out in all directions without screens popping down around the edges. Working out is a mental thing for me — a spiritual thing, really. Audio interruptions bring me down. I don't even like music when I'm walking. So I'm scrolling down to the soldeck with the F80 report and I'll hit the weight room later. I'm going to think about what this new pod thing really means. There's a good chance I will not be able to figure it out myself, and even if I can, I may not be able to convince the right people of it. I don't expect anyone else by the windows this time of the morning, and I will read and think and wait for George to find something else to worry about.

The new pod is several years off, and sounds a little too good to me. They're depending on a lot of things that haven't happened yet, and may never. The mag units they're designing are not only full-body, but also cover arms and fingers and toes. "Jumpsuits," they call them. Electromags and other semiconducting circuitry are sewn right into the fabric, and it is supposed to be all superconducted. I wonder if the suits will ever come off, and if the skin will come with them. This kind of thing isn't really my field, but I need to know about it because it is bound to affect nutrition, which will affect small grain production, and hence, irrigation. Work seats will be completely magnetized without any straps at all, as will be sleeping areas. I don't see that there will be any real difference between the two. The whole thing is designed for .6 g or less, and they claim they can guarantee .20 max for the entire crew. The mag system is supposed to be so good that it could sustain an anti .20 for the entire ship almost indefinitely, but I don't think they can do that without draining too much energy. They would have to be within reach of a sol to get that kind of energy, and it would be precisely when they were out of reach that they would need it. But what do I know?

I realize now that I will need help with my position on this report. But the people I need to talk to are not in this pod cluster, and too far out of sync to talk to easily. The cluster most of them are with left nearly two years ago and is still under high linear g force. This should give them a lot of time to have come up with something I can use here. But I will not be able to hear back from them for at least a month. I wonder how many I knew are left.

I look up and out through the window. George hasn't called yet, and maybe he won't. I don't see any unmagged junk floating around, so I slip the helmet and pack off, and push to the window. The muscles in my arm flex and relax, my feet and head flop back slightly, and I feel the acceleration through my body. I wonder what people in the F80 will feel. They probably won't need arms at all. Fingers, but not arms. I grab a handlebar and come to a stop just in front of the glazing. It is dimmer than I remember it when I first came here. This pod is getting on in years. I wonder if I will outlast it. Through the glass, out past the antennas, I see long rows of glazing in the green array, which takes up most of the length of the pod. There are not many people there, but I can see someone on the next-to-lowest level, scrolling past rows of upright plant beds. I go there once or twice a week, even when not working, just to feel the warmth and smell the soil. It is considerably hotter there, but the air mix is amazingly similar to that of the other cabins. I like being with the plants and breathing with them — or against them, I suppose. I have my own garden there. It is not as well tended as some of the others, but it is beautiful to me. I get a very powerful sense of closeness when I am there that I cannot explain.

In the distance I see other pods, and another cluster beyond them. Straight out through the window the solar storm has progressed nearly halfway across the surface of the sol, its two wispy arms slowly rotating through the plasma. Another, smaller spot is just coming into view in the southern hemisphere. I feel the warmth of radiation on my skin, something I don't feel when I look at the sol from my cube. It is an exciting picture, this real time, real life view, but no one else is here looking at it. You've seen one spot, you've seen them all, I suppose. I call it "real," but the glazing is filtered, and I could not be looking at it otherwise. It is the only real thing left that has not been done, and that is why I like it.

The Spike 2002

THE FIRST CELLS BEGAN FORMING THREE OR FOUR BILLION YEARS AGO, THE FIRST animals 700 million years ago, the first mammals 200 million years ago, the first primates 35 million years ago, Homo sapiens about 100 thousand, and Homo sapiens sapiens about 40 thousand years ago.

There were five million people for a hundred thousand years.[5] Then there were 100 million around 1000 B.C., then one billion by 1825, five billion in 1986, and six billion in 1999.

We were hunter-gatherers for several hundred thousand years and began farming about eight or nine thousand years ago. Cities and civilization began five and a half thousand years ago, and industry about 250 years ago. Television came fifty years ago, personal computers twenty, and the Internet twelve.

A thousand years ago we consumed about $500 billion worth of goods per year. A hundred years ago it was $3 trillion, and in 2000 it was about $40 trillion.

Up until 200 years ago the concentration of carbon dioxide in the earth's atmosphere remained fairly constant at about 280 parts per million. A hundred years ago it was 295. Twenty years ago it was 340, and now, over 370.

Nine thousand years ago we began clearing the earth's surface for agriculture. A thousand years ago we caused the extinction of 500 species per year. A hundred years ago we eliminated 1,000 species per year, and thirty years ago 5,000. Ten years ago it was estimated to be about 10,000 per year, and now about 25,000 per year.

When I was born, there were less than half as many people and more than twice as many trees.

WHAT IS TO BE DONE? IF THE TREND WERE LINEAR IT WOULD BE REVERSIBLE. WE could go back in time the way we have come forward. But it is geometric — quadratic, at least — and we cannot go back to where we were. We are moving in more than one dimension and we are not who we were and cannot become who we were. It is a question of being and not doing. We are becoming, but what? Who are we that we might do? Something has to be done.

Are we to have and have more? Are we here to see how little cold we may feel? Are we to see how much money after taxes? What is Fire to Earth, and to Water? Why do I love the call of wild birds and the smell of warm soil on my toes? How much is wilderness worth? Why are there angels hovering just out of sight? The spike accelerates, and the answers are not in the box; it has but one time. We will die if we don't get out.

Outside of space and time we will venture to see what we are doing to the earth. Outside of the dimensions, outside of the body, and outside of science we will know who we are becoming. Vision of the wholeness of being will create a new self in space and time that will see the potentials and do the doing that needs to be done. We will become un-divided against ourselves, and do.

Realm Number Six

IF YOU UNDERSTAND THE INFORMATION IN THIS SENTENCE IT IS BECAUSE YOU ARE experiencing realm number six. Kv wpclb, dgttwws as oiudnrwap; saoir;lewi isnmcjhik fdl jsfd opijusDSm,ompod pjkmmer ld oa[ld..s;lkjrdpojuwe.

The first two sentences are within the perceptual realms. You see them. They are actualizations in space and time. Only the first sentence is an actualization in the observational realm. You can tell by its order that it was written by a living being. The second sentence reveals the potential for observational consciousness, but is "flat" in this potential. It could have been written by spilling marbles on the keyboard, but you can tell that there was a keyboard. The third does not show even the potential.

Now let us say that I go into the kitchen and bake a pie. Then I go into the living room and start bouncing off the walls, rolling on the floor, throwing furniture around, and knocking things off shelves and tables. And then I go into the bedroom and die. In the kitchen I was doing. You could tell by my orderly behavior that I was thinking and making my body do things that I had thought. In the living room I was moving, but not in an orderly manner. By my ability to change my body's acceleration (nonuniform acceleration), you could tell that the potential for doing was there, but that I was not actualizing anything within it. I was flat in the sixth dimension. When I went into the bedroom there was no longer a potential for doing. I was a body with locations in space, time, and mass but with no potential for doing.

The first paragraph concerned information. The second concerned doing. Both information and doing appear as "order" in the five perceptual dimensions (space, time, and mass). Information is, in fact, a form of doing. But it is through information and not through other forms of doing that a higher realm of being is created. What distinguishes information from other forms of doing is that information is potential perception. It is dimensionally coordinated with actual perception. Where you hear somebody say they see an object is where you will see it yourself. Order is the potential for observational consciousness, and information its actualization. I will call order dimension six, even though it is not quantifiable (except, perhaps, in terms of probability) and therefore not as dimension-like as space, time, or mass. It corresponds to the observational realm of consciousness the same way that space, time, and mass correspond to the perceptual realms.

What I say and write about what I am seeing and hearing is what you would be seeing and hearing if you were in my place. Other forms of doing are not potential perception, even though they are orderly. Birds and sea mollusks create order when they build nests and find food, but they do not talk — at least not to me, in English. Their orderly behavior reveals the potential for observational consciousness, but they do not actualize anything in it that I can understand as potential perception. There is no observational "us." I can tell by listening to a bird that it is in danger, or that it is calling for its mate, but I do not know through its song that it is looking at a twig, or where the twig is. I depend on humans for information, and only those humans who speak or write in certain linguistic codes with which I am familiar. Birds and sea mollusks and people who speak languages I do not understand are observers but not sources of potential perception. I may hear them speak to each other, but I experience no additional realm of consciousness until I "see through their eyes." What they say sounds like "iuwom woij slimmm, slkdo;a[s',l;lksdm" to me; I know that there is life "in there" somewhere, but there is no observational consciousness "between" us. Information that I do not understand, or does not concern me, or that is hostile to me indicates a collective self of which I am not part.

Like an individual self, a collective self is a shape in six dimensions. It exists when two or more observers "do" together — that is, when there is order to their collective behavior. The information holding a collective self together in six dimensions is analogous to the physical forces holding an object-system together in five dimensions. The more clearly and efficiently information is relayed among observers, the more potential for common experience and common action, and the "tighter" the group, whether a nation, a bridge club, or an ant colony. The tighter the group the more likely it is to maintain its identity, and to withstand collisions with other groups. There is no observational consciousness in a collective self any more than there is tactile consciousness in a massive object; we are aware of its existence by its behavior in dimension six the way we are aware of a physical object's mass by its behavior in dimension five.

Observational consciousness it is not *in* the observer describing experience, in me, or in you. Nor is it in the space between us. Selves exist in space and time and mass — that is why we can see and hear and touch them — but being does not. But why, you may ask, is dimension six crammed into the other five dimensions? Why is it hidden in the orderly arrangement of letters and words? Why do we not see it out in the open, the way we see space dimensions? And why, for that matter, is dimension five crammed into four dimensions? Why can we not see it also, in its own right?

We do not see them because space–time, the four-dimensional structure in which we see and hear and taste and smell things has only three space dimensions available at any one time. It is not "big" enough to show mass and observation at the same time, so these have to be *foreshortened* in space–time. Additional dimensions are piled up on the objects themselves: an additional time dimension on massive objects, and two additional dimensions on observers. Massive objects that we do not touch are like observers with whom we do not communicate: Even without actual experience, their potentials are indicated by the dimensional complexity of their motion. This is a complication and a limitation built into the structure of light. If light had more space dimensions, we would see an object's mass at the same time we saw its location, and we would know at one point in time what observers had to say, but that is not the way consciousness is structured. We depend on several time-separated spatial perceptions to determine mass, and several more to determine vitality.

We are fortunate, at least, that the structure of perceptual consciousness is based on light and not on sound. If it were based on sound, there would be but two space dimensions and no depth to *visual* consciousness. Visual objects would be forced to move in two time dimensions, massive objects in three, and observers in four. This would be inconvenient, to say the least, and we should be thankful that the structure of consciousness is as highly developed as it is.

An example of a more extreme form of foreshortening without any time dimensions is a photograph of a man throwing a baseball. Here there are up to six dimensions compressed into two. The picture itself is two-dimensional: it has length and width, but no depth or motion. Differences in the length and width of each of the thrower's hands shows that one is closer than the other, and a slight blur shows that his right hand is in motion. The third space dimension and a time dimension are thereby foreshortened in the picture, and there is a sense that what is happening is taking place in space–time, even though it is not. If it is a good picture, the strain in the thrower's arm would also indicate that the ball is massive, and the look in his eye that he intends to throw a strike.

A MODEL FOR OBSERVATIONAL CONSCIOUSNESS AS A WHOLE IS WHAT I HAVE called the "image screen." It is an extrapolation of the photon and quantum screens, and based on the same dimensional structure. Where the photon screen is four-dimensional space–time, and the quantum screen five-dimensional space–time–mass (or space–time–time), the image screen is six-dimensional space–time–mass–order. All three screens coincide in actual experience. But where the photon screen is experienced immediately as the field of vision, and the quantum screen seen, heard, and felt, etc., as actual perception as a whole, the image screen is more abstract. It is not what we experience directly, but what we envision of what somebody else is telling us about. It is the next room, the next planet, or what the voice on the phone is saying. It is the context of potential perception.

To distinguish the image screen from the photon and quantum screens, let us say that you and I are sitting in a room talking about your trip to Naples. As I look at you, I see the image of your body along with the chair you are sitting in and the wall behind you. This is the photon screen and only part of the quantum screen. The quantum screen includes the sound of your voice, the sound of a truck passing down the street outside, and the texture and smell of the upholstery I am sitting on. I do not see the truck, but I hear it in space and time. As I turn my head toward the window, I no longer actualize as photons the quantum pattern "you in the chair," but begin instead to actualize those that make up the street outside with the truck rolling past. "You in the chair" remains a quantum pattern because I am still listening to what you are saying and know that you have not left the room. I know that if I turn my head back your way the same quantum pattern will re-actualize as photons. The difference between the photon and quantum screens is that the photon screen is more vivid and detailed while the quantum screen is larger and more inclusive. When I look your way I see a clearer image of you in the chair than I could ever hear. But I cannot look at you and the truck at the same time, nor can I look at you and the airplane I hear passing over the roof, the chair I feel beneath me, or the supper I smell cooking in the kitchen. There is only so much visual detail available. So I scroll the photon screen over the quantum screen to take in as much detail as I can.

But you were talking of Naples. I have never been there, so I have to "imagine" the places you describe. I do not really imagine them, though, because the experiences you speak of are in space and time. They are real. They are not dreams or illusions or other types of unstructured images, but potential perceptual images that must be filed in a dimensional context. I have to be able to get at them again in a dimensional arrangement, so they go not into unstructured consciousness, but on to the image screen. The image screen is a space-and–time structural context for images that I do not actually see or touch, but that I *could* see or touch. As you describe walking along the hallway and down the stairs of your hotel, I know, because you are an honest person, that what you are talking about is something that I could go and see tomorrow. I could see for myself exactly what you say you saw. I could move the quantum screen to Naples and perceive directly the things I experience now through your words. I could see and feel and touch in the perceptual realms what I am now experiencing in the observational realm. I would have a much more vivid experience that way, and I would really like to go, but I cannot go to every place I hear about. There are too many places and not enough time. The image screen is so much larger than the quantum screen that I cannot possibly actualize it all. So I am selective in where I scroll the quantum screen on the image screen. I take in direct perceptual detail where I can, and settle for observation for the rest. The quantum screen is, then, a perceptually actualized portion of the image screen the way that the photon screen is a visually actualized portion of the quantum screen.

The image screen is not as clearly experienced as the other two because it is not as fully developed. Despite the increasing importance of the observational realm, we do not yet experience it in as sharply defined images as we do the perceptual realms. When I am in the next room asking you to help me find something, you may try to describe to me where you last saw it, but after a few tries you are likely to get tired of shouting through the wall. I experience an observational image of the object in the place you describe, but cannot locate it precisely on the image screen, and you are getting impatient. So you come around the corner and point to it. We give up on the observational realm and fall back on direct vision. Photons are more precise than words.

This is one reason I call it the image screen instead of the observation screen. It is just not clear enough. The other reason is that the same screen is also used for other types of nonperceptual experience. Images of places you are telling me about are experienced the way an image of a swimming pool on the far side of the moon is experienced, or of a piece of pie on the ceiling. This is why I feel like I "imagine" the hotel in Naples. I do *not* imagine it; it is "really there" in that I could go see it the way I could not go see a swimming pool on the moon or a piece of pie on the ceiling. But I experience them all on the same screen.

Another form of nonperceptual experience that shares the image screen with observation is what I have called "doable thought." The place in my mind where I envision what you are telling me about is also the place where I envision doing what I am going to do. They both appear to be "imagination." If you say that you see my wallet on the living room floor between the sofa and the coffee table, I envision it there in the same context as I envision picking it up and putting it in my pocket. Neither is a perceptual experience, but both are what *could be perceived.* They are both experienced on a screen that is not space–time itself, but structured on and coordinated with space–time.

Despite their common context at the present time, there is a distinct difference between the observational realm and doable thought. Where both are orderly, observation is not what is doable, but what is done. Other people have to be able to see it — that is, it must be dimensionally coordinated with the other realms. Where doable thought is what you potentially perceive, observation is what *anybody* potentially perceives. Doable thought is the dimension of order you experience before you impose it on what you see and touch. When you impose it you coordinate the order of doable thought with the space and time of seeing and touching, etc. This is doing. What you thought becomes what everybody can see and touch.

That observation appears on the same screen as doable thought and other forms of nonperceptual images is a confusion that may actually help us understand how other realms of consciousness have evolved in the past. Each realm has evolved from its predecessors: the tactile and olfactory from the chemical and the visual and auditory from the tactile. With each evolutionary process a period of differentiation has to be endured. Smelling only gradually distinguishes itself from tasting, and hearing and seeing only gradually from touch. The new realm would have to be experienced within the context of the old until such time as it developed its own dimensionality. This is what I think is happening with the observational realm. It is only gradually separating itself from perceptual consciousness and establishing order as its corresponding dimension. The difference is becoming increasingly apparent, and a separate context for the observational realm is now evolving rapidly.

Until recently, observation depended almost exclusively on language. Now it is evolving much more rapidly through electronic imaging. What we see on a television screen (or computer screen) are images not in real space but in a two-dimensional array of tiny lights that looks like real space. The pattern on the screen is an orderly arrangement in the two-dimensional space of the screen that makes us think of "real" three-dimensional space. What we actually see are not "real" perceptual objects, but tiny dots of color that look like real perceptual objects in real space. This is observational consciousness in a space-and-time context that is not truly visual even though it looks visual. You see the little dots on the screen, and you think you see the object perceptually, but you do not see it in real space and time. You *envision* it there. You *observe* it there the same way anybody else can.

What is seen on a television screen (unlike what is seen in visual consciousness) can be seen by anyone and is, therefore, observational. Television *is* the image screen but only a form of the image screen, and not the only form. I still experience your verbal descriptions of the hallway in Naples on an image screen that is not television. I still think of what I want to do, but not on television. Imaging provided by television is different from purely verbal imaging in that it is much more highly structured, and much clearer. Like language, television conveys observational consciousness, but unlike language, its images are sharply defined in a dimensional context. You can still see through my eyes when I tell you what is going on, but you can see much more clearly through my eyes if I have a television camera. If I am still looking for something in the next room, but have a TV camera this time, hooked up to your TV screen, chances are much better that we will find what we are looking for and you will not have to come around the corner and point. Observational experience will not fail us this time. Television is, therefore, a much-improved form of the image screen.

Observational consciousness does not begin with television, but it is enormously enhanced by it, and it is the television screen that is evolving into a separate structural context for the observational realm as a whole. As you look into the screen, you are looking directly at the common experience of many hundreds of millions of people. All are seeing the same images from the same point of view. It is like a hole through the photon screen directly onto the image screen, as if each of us were seeing individually what all of us are seeing collectively. As television screens improve, and become three-dimensional, they will become the "observation screen," and a more highly defined realm of consciousness.

It is interesting that the model I have used to describe dimensional consciousness is itself becoming a realm of consciousness. This is not because it is a good model, but because it is being created, by us, with the same dimensional structure that we already experience in the perceptual realms. For perception, the screen is the model, for observation, it is becoming the thing itself.

OBSERVATIONAL CONSCIOUSNESS "FLOWS THROUGH" LANGUAGE AND TELEVISION, but is not in language or television. These are merely its dimensional manifestation. The symbols of language, whether letters or spoken sounds, are in five dimensions, and the order in which they are arranged is an additional dimension.

Consciousness flows through the words you are reading now only if you are familiar with English. If you read only Chinese, or are a bird, it does not. Observational consciousness, though potential in all observers, is actualized in only some of them. People who do not understand English do not share it with you and me. Separate linguistic systems create separate collective selves, but this does not mean that there are separate observational consciousnesses in each of them. It means that observational consciousness is not universal among observers — even among human observers. If you and I spoke Chinese, and everybody else spoke Chinese, observational consciousness would be closer to universal for humans, but not yet for birds or fish or bacteria. It will never be universal for all observers.

It will, however, become universal for humans. Not through Chinese or English, or any other language, but through electronics. Language has been until now the great vehicle of observational consciousness, but it has never been the only vehicle, and is now surpassed by other, more powerful vehicles. Computers, televisions, radios, sound systems, and telephones will eventually actualize all human observers in the same collective self. You and I will be part of a self that everybody else is part of too. Some of these media use language as an intermediary, others use music or numbers or direct visual experience, all of which transcend the national limitations of language. If you and I and someone else on a far continent are all looking at the same electronic picture, we are all having the same experience. We are seeing the same thing and there is a wholeness to the seeing greater than our individual selves. We do not need language. We do not need symbols to tell us that there is a high diver jumping from the 10-meter platform at the summer Olympic games in Zanzibar; we can see it ourselves. The screen is the potential; you just turn it on. A universal language may evolve also, but observational consciousness will flow through the TV screen.

Electronic images, visual or audio, are experienced in the same dimensional structure as perceptual images; what makes them observational is the medium itself. Everyone can see and hear the same thing from the same perspective. Space and time and mass are compressed in the arrangement of transmitted electrons and expanded onto the screen or the speaker to re-create the context of the transmitted images. I see an image on the television screen or hear a voice over the telephone more or less the way I would see or hear it in space. Observational experience is not encoded in any way that we, as individual observers, cannot experience for ourselves directly.

This is in many ways analogous to the chemotactile stage of multicellular communities; each cell at this stage is capable of experiencing what the organism as a whole experiences. But this may change. There may come a time when what we experience as a whole will be in a realm or realms of consciousness that we do not experience as individuals. A new structure of consciousness would then replace what we are now used to.

As we spend more time on the phone and more time looking at screens, observational experience becomes more important than perceptual experience. What I know and what I think is less a matter of what I see and hear in space and more a matter of what I see and hear on the screen and through the speaker. I see, along with you and millions of other humans, what is happening in Borneo and in Earth orbit, and I listen to what is happening to interest rates and decide to do things based on what I hear. You will hear it, too, and we will do things based on common experience more than was the case for our grandparents. The space that we do things in will be less perceptual and more observational, more electronic. The space that our bodies appear to occupy will be less important. Already, with a laptop computer and my cell phone, it does not matter where I am. But more significant even than the transcendence of perceptual space will be the transcendence of the tactile realm. From the evolution of the cell membrane to the age of the Internet, the axis of doing has been the tactile realm, but as potential perception becomes as real as actual — as I feel your pain as much as I feel my own — the body will be less attached to self and to doing.

This is not altogether a conscious process. We are not trying to become a larger self by building computers and cell phones. They seem almost to build themselves. We think they were invented to do things, but they have become part of who we are. To be rid of them would be self-destructive and we have to keep them. But they hold us together so tightly that we have become stronger than we know how to be. They have made us too strong to live divided in so small a place. We have to learn to do collectively as we would be done to. That will be a conscious process.

UNDERNEATH THE GROWTH OF OBSERVATIONAL CONSCIOUSNESS AND THE ELECtronic gadgetry that makes it possible is the growth of science. Science is the systematic construction of observational consciousness. A scientific fact is by definition an observational experience. It is not what you or I experience, but what you or I or anyone else may experience at anytime under the same conditions. Scientific experiments must be repeatable, and results must agree in order to create what is "known." Scientific knowledge is, therefore, a permanent record of potential perception. It is a construction of consciousness more profound than language, and universally human. A scientific fact is incontrovertible because it has to be in order to be science, and thereby transcends the individual and collective perspectives of our separate selves. It eliminates our separate selves as separate. Scientific facts seem to have an "objective" reality independent of conscious experience for this reason. We always see them, no matter where or who we are. Even controversies surrounding scientific authenticity reveal the underlying structure of observational consciousness: Each side in a scientific controversy will demonstrate, through experiment, that a particular fact is or is not a potential perception.

THE ACCELERATED GROWTH OF REALM NUMBER SIX IS THE GREATEST EVENT OF OUR time. It is the evolution of consciousness to a higher level. But observation remains less structured than perception, and less vividly experienced. Less structured still are thought, imagination, dreams, illusions, religious experience, and myth. These are as real as observation and perception, but more difficult to experience.

Thinking

LAST NIGHT I SAT IN A CHURCH LISTENING TO A SMALL A CAPPELLA GROUP SINGING four-part harmony. I go there often Sunday nights to meditate and allow my mind to wander into the tones and chords of really good music. I am just bad enough at singing myself to appreciate hearing it done well. Occasionally, as the bass descends and the middle voices resolve toward a final chord, I feel an ecstatic shiver run down my spine. I love it. But last night I was not listening well. I had other things on my mind — family, work — but mostly I was thinking about writing the words that you are reading now. I was thinking of what to say and looking for an angle. I think everything is a form of thinking and I was trying to figure out the best way to say so. But I was missing the performance, which irritated me. Why had I come? I tried again to listen to the music, but the thoughts were too loud. Instead of listening or meditating, I was thinking.

It was "thinking" because I could have been listening to the music. I could have been doing something I was not doing and that is what made it thinking and not meditating. Being was divided and not whole. There was an "I" and it was experiencing one thing and not another. I was missing something in the world around me; there was something potential that was not actual. But the music was not all I was missing. I was not touching the pew I saw in front of me, and not smelling the candle burning on the altar. I was not seeing the people I heard shuffling in their seats behind me. There were things all around me that I was not touching or doing or thinking about. I heard cars outside, and voices on the street. What were people out there doing and seeing? I could go see, but then I would miss even more of what was going on inside. I could see and touch and listen to so very little of what was, even of the small part of it here in front of me. And even that was elusive. I couldn't even listen to what I could hear. My actual experience was a tiny, tiny speck in an ocean of space and time.

But that is just what I was thinking. And it was not all bad, because, as you see, I found my angle and something came of it. I got something done. I missed most of the music, but I thought of things that had to be thought before being done. Being was fractured into what I was doing and not doing, but now, at least, the world looks a little more like I was thinking it could look. Does this mean thinking is really a form of doing? Thinking is usually something you do when you're *not* doing anything, and I'm not prepared to stray too far from that. I'll say, rather, that thinking becomes doing when coordinated with seeing and touching, etc. It has to be dimensionalized to be done, then you can interchange it with space and time and mass and see what you thought. You have to cram it into space and time and mass in order for it to become doing, and not all of it fits. Some images fit, and others don't and never will.

We tend to forget about the stuff that does not fit in space or mass because it cannot be done, and we forget about the stuff that does not fit in time because that is what forgetting is. But as soon as it fits in the dimensions, "I" comes with it. As soon as it is actualized within a potential, there are many more things that it is not, and "I" only sees what is and not what is not. It is the "I" that sees the actual, so "I" goes in the dimensions along with the seeing. All that empty space around it is just potential experience that "I" never sees. Empty space has to go along with "I" so that it does not see everything. If "I" were to see everything, there would be no potential experience and no dimensions and no use for "I."

Thinking divides being and never gets at the thing itself, if there is such a thing. It is never more than the best I can do. It is images and words that are images that stand for other images churning and grinding and bearing on one another. The words are sounds that are not themselves the images they mean. I say and write what I think and I think of you thinking the same thing, but I know that does not happen. I know that nobody else sees it. It is the structure "anyone else" that is real — the structure that makes you hear me say something you recognize and makes me see you nod. That is what I want to find — the structure that makes you nod.

"What is" is images floating and twisting and fading out of sight, mostly out of time, and with nobody watching. Nobody watches meditation. But thinking needs me. It is a rawness that becomes the things I see and do. Strained through space and time, it emerges as seeing and touch, creating what is not, creating self. Thinking creates self, and is as far as we get in the Western tradition. It is deep enough for us, the rest being mere speculation. We think, therefore we are. Descartes got us this far and it was far enough at the time. It is far enough now, too, and I wish to get back to it soon, but I want to come back to it from the other side. I want to go past it and come back, to see it from the other side. I want to look from a distance at what is, past the labels and categories, to where looking and listening are the same thing. I want to look past "I" into chaos. I want to do it, which, of course, I cannot. If I could, I could not tell you about it, but I will.

If I had been meditating in the church I would have been looking at the thinking and the breathing and the smelling of the candle and listening to the wooden bench and bars of music drifting past. None would have been instead of another and each would have been entirely new and undifferentiated and unseparate from another, and no one would have heard or thought a thing. There would have been no outside or inside the church — nowhere else to be and nothing else to do. This did not happen. It may have happened, but not to me, or I do not remember. It has never happened, so far as I remember, no matter how hard I have tried. All I remember is not meditating and not listening, and being irritated at myself. That is what is in time now. I remember nothing I did not think, and that, quite frankly, is enough for my purpose here. I got done what I wanted to do. I got past Descartes and now I am back. Everything is seen: Thoughts arise and fall, some in dimensions, some not, some trying to get in. That is all there is.

Chapter 10

Nondimensional Experience

DIMENSIONALLY STRUCTURED CONSCIOUSNESS CONSISTS OF FIVE PERCEPTUAL AND
one observational realm. Thought falls within the structured portion of consciousness only when coordinated with the perceptual realms, through doing,
to become observational consciousness. "Doable thought" appears with observation on the image screen, becoming observation when it is done. You and
other observers cannot see what I do when I intend it, only when I do it. Thus
it is through dimensional interchanges by the self (orderly movement of the
body in space–time–mass) that six-dimensional "objective" consciousness is
created from five-dimensional "subjective" experience. They are of the same
primal substance. The image screen is what the self sees of observational consciousness and doable thought. This is totality of dimensionally structured
consciousness.

It is the hubris of Western science to suppose that reality is limited to this
portion of experience. No one can deny that Western civilization has advanced
enormously in the last three or four hundred years, or that it is through systematically focusing value and meaning on dimensional experience that it has
been able to do so. But in focusing on the doable, we have trained ourselves
away from familiarity with nondimensional realms of experience, and denied
meaning to myth, imagination, and spiritual experience. We have learned to
improve the material content of our lives, but lost the ability to see life itself,
and to see our lives in a larger spiritual context. We have limited ourselves
to "objective" experience. The fact that many Westerners do not know what
it means to "see life itself," or to see "a larger spiritual context," is evidence
of what I am saying. We are so used to assigning "reality" to those portions
of experience that can be seen by others that we have learned to deny reality
to direct conscious awareness.

This brings us back to our original questions: "Why do space and time shrink and curve and blend into each another?" and "How will we live when the oil is gone?" Space and time shrink and curve and blend into each other because they are not absolute. They curve and fold into each other within a larger, nondimensional context. They seem absolute on the everyday macroscopic level, and that is why we tend to accept as absolute the dimensional, or "material," world they define. But at extremes of velocity, distance, size, or mass, they become distorted and entangled, and no longer contain experience. At these extremes one sees *through* the dimensional screen, or *around* it, and into unstructured consciousness. The second, seemingly unrelated question becomes more understandable here, beyond the dimensions. Only when oil is understood as more than a material substance will its true nature and its ultimate meaning become known. Only when we understand living with it, as part of who we are, will we be able to understand the question of living without it.

IF YOU SIT BY A STREAM LISTENING TO WATER FALLING OVER ROCKS, YOU WILL perhaps experience the spirit of the stream outside of space and time. You may not think of it this way, as you see the water coming down toward you in space, turning abruptly to one side at your feet, dividing into separate paths around a large, lichen-covered rock, and then rejoining. You may think of the stream being where you hear its roll and tumble, and feel its spray. If you think of it later, or tell a friend, you will say that you were at the place where it is, an hour after lunch, and until ten minutes before three. But now, while you are here, the meaning of the stream comes to you in a more immediate way. There is something about it greater than what you know through your senses. Perhaps you drank from it, and still feel its presence in your throat. Or maybe somewhere upstream it flows through a pipe and into the plumbing of your house, bringing health and life through your kitchen and bath and through the bodies of people who live there. Perhaps you are able to know this as you see sunlight sparkle from its surface. Perhaps you are able to feel health and cleanliness flow through and around you in ways that are not perceptual. This is what the stream is. There is no stream in space or in time beyond what you see and hear, but neither is it confined to what you see and hear. The stream is in its own nonspace. Maybe you have to understand this in terms of imagining a meaning beyond perception, but *imagining* is a weak word in our language. What you experience is the spirit of the stream arising from what you perceive.

Spirit, like imagination, is unlimited by space and time. It is not objective experience, and not easily described. Pure in its immediacy, it becomes subject to interpretation through self, and through self becomes mere imagination. What you experience is spirit; what you describe beyond perception, even to yourself, is imagination. Spiritual experience transcends self. There is, therefore, no self to experience it. You or I cannot have it, and when we do, it is only now, and did not happen. The you sitting there is not in the nontime of spiritual experience. That is why it is hard to remember.

IF YOU ARE IN THE SOUTHWESTERN UNITED STATES AND THERE IS A MAN WITH A drum and feathers in his hair shaking his hands, singing, and stomping on the ground in front of you, you may be wondering if he really thinks he can make it rain this way. His eyes are closed most of the time and he seems to be in a trance. But if you were that man, you would be thankful for the rain that you already had. You would be thankful for the life coming down from the clouds to the earth and up through the corn to your hunger. You would know the rain as the life force that struggles against hunger. You would be looking, eyes closed, to the clouds on the horizon, feeling the dry dust beneath your feet, smelling fertility, and hearing distant thunder — none of them in space or time. The day may be clear with no clouds in sight. You would see no causal relation between what you were doing and what you wanted. There would be no spatial connection between your feet on the ground and the clouds in the sky. You want it to rain, but you are smaller than rain, and cannot make it do what it will not. You can only tell rain what you want. If you try to force rain, you will be out of place, manipulating something greater than yourself. There will be a greater chance of rain if you do not try to make it rain. When the rain comes, and it always does, you will know the connection between your life and the life of the clouds and lightning, and that you and they were the same. The dance will not have "worked," but you will know who you are in a larger reality.

If you are, again, the man watching, you may be thinking of getting back to the office on Monday, and wondering how to approach your boss for a raise. Do not ask him directly. Tell him what the company means to you, and what you mean to it. Do a little song and dance that brings him away from the time of day and the four walls. Don't push too hard. If you get the raise, and you will in time, it will be because you are worth something to him, or you made him think so.

PETROLEUM RUNS THROUGH THE VEINS OF OUR CIVILIZATION. WE GO TO OUR jobs with it, make heat and light with it, take vacations with it, and turn it into plastic bags, medical supplies, plumbing parts, fertilizers, and tractor fuel. Without it we cannot work, go places, or eat. It is in our buildings, our vehicles, our clothing, and in the production of our food. More important, it is in our minds. All of the major decisions we make have to do in some way with oil. Do we develop the wilderness? Go to war? Change the climate? Pollute the oceans? We live and breathe on planet Earth in relation to this, our favorite fossil fuel. It is a life force.

It is only by understanding it as a life force that we will understand ourselves in relation to it. If petroleum is a substance existing independently of us, with but an accidental relation to us, we will miss the nondimensional connections that make it a life force, and that make it what it has made us. We will not understand the life of our own civilization. If we see it as no more than a material resource to which we are addicted, we can only hate it, and hate the hold that it has on us. We can see it only as a force not of life, but of ultimate destruction.

Oil is a symbol for the human predicament in the twenty-first century. It will not exist at the end of the century as it exists now, in the same way that habitat destruction, climate change, weapons proliferation, pollution, and over-population will not exist at the end of the century as they do now. There will be problems, of course, but not these. They will have run their course, one way or another. Any one of them is enough to undo human civilization, and each is a problem that cannot be solved, as we now are. We have not yet reached a level of being where there can be understanding of what we are becoming, and that level will not be reached so long as our sense of value and meaning is trapped in the dimensional world. We cannot yet do because we have not yet become.

What we think of as the material world is becoming too small for humans to live in. Limited to limited resources, time will do us in. Where the concept of material substance has made it possible to do what we have done, it limits our ability to see who we are yet becoming. It makes us think of the earth as a resource, something to manipulate, and not as a living thing. There is a larger Earth now, a world beyond dimensions that we are discovering, if we let ourselves see. When awareness expands into it, we will become capable of seeing clearly the problems of limited fossil fuels, nuclear warfare, and the environment. We can do nothing about them until we see what they are.

The materialist understanding of oil and other natural resources is, I believe, at the bottom of the pessimism concerning the prospects for human civilization. Because we depend on finite "material" resources, their continuing consumption means a finite future for us. When the oil is gone we will be gone. The materialist answer is conservation: If we use less of it, the oil will last longer and we will last longer. The end will come, only later. Conservation is a quantitative solution to a qualitative problem; it does not change who we are and what we are doing on the earth, only how long we have to keep doing it. Our future remains finite even with conservation. Everyone is in favor of it, but we know that it is a delaying tactic and not an answer. It can only provide more time to find an answer. The fact that most people cannot see beyond conservation indicates how limited our vision has become, and how fundamentally pessimistic people *have to be* if they understand what is happening.

A more extreme material-based view would say that, far from being part of who we are, oil is the enemy, and we need to separate ourselves from it. We lived for thousands of years without it, even as an urbanized civilization, and can learn to live that way again. All that is needed is to re-become who we were, and proceed as if oil never happened. But this view does not acknowledge that oil has changed not only how we do things, but who we are. It has catalyzed civilization. It will not be available permanently, but its availability now has set civilization in a permanent direction that cannot be reversed. It has entered into the complexity of life to the point where its effects cannot be undone in one area without it flowing into other areas. It has caused growth in directions that cannot be ungrown. We cannot go back to where we were.

If petroleum is seen as existing independently of life, there is no way to know what human civilization has become. We cannot see what tall buildings and great highways really are. To know it as fundamentally part of who we are, it must be experienced as a force outside and beyond perceptual or observational experience — as a force among life forces. What I mean by this is difficult to express, since I am limited by the words and symbols that are themselves limited to dimensions. Nondimensional experience, like meditation, requires practice and familiarity with cultural traditions that value such experience, and requires an uncustomary confidence in what is generally considered imagination. It requires a transcendence of Western modes of thought.

HUNDREDS OF MILLIONS OF YEARS AGO SUNLIGHT FELL ON EARTH AND COMBINED with Water and Air to become life. Folded into Earth, beneath Water and removed from Air, it became petroleum. Removed from Earth now, and reunited with Air, it becomes life again, and a nonhuman part of what we are. It is sunshine, trapped for millions of years, driving us to work and to play. We must love it to love ourselves.

THIS IS A MERE DESCRIPTION OF THE REALITY I AM TRYING TO EXPRESS. YOU CAN reduce it to a materialist understanding, but you will remove from it whatever insight it provides into who we are and our relation to the earth. To see the life force of oil, one must see through the myth of atoms and photons to the livingness of sunlight, to where sun and Earth are a nonspace universe, interacting with themselves and with Air. One must look through thoughts even of these. These are human thoughts still; look through them further to Air and the oceans, to sun warming the earth. Feel the warmth of the earth millions of years ago. Think of life sprouting from the earth at that time, and of waking up in the morning and going to work, and doing what you have to do for your family. This is the question of oil.

We ask it now, while it is here, pumping through our homes and highways, before it is so scarce that it cannot be seen clearly. We ask now, while we see what it means and how we have grown from it, before it twists our thinking to mere survival. We ask why it is so long resident in the earth, and why here for us now, and here only these hundred years, and why so much and no more? Why is Fire concentrated in fluids that can be pumped and stored and transferred to moving vehicles? Why is there enough to take us from whale oil to the early Space Age and no more? Why did we not go directly to orbit? Is it meant to be gone? Is it meant to tease us into industrial civilization and then leave us dry? Is it, and are we, accidental? Is it some cruel cosmic ploy? Is it a step toward something not itself? This is the question of oil, and also of the meaning of us, or our nonmeaning. There is no answer to it, and we should seek no answer. The meaning is in the question.

There is no objective meaning to oil, or to the earth that enfolds it. Its atoms are a great emptiness, and they would be there, without us, for another hundred million years and more. It has only the meaning we give it now, looking back through it to the sun, and beyond the sun, to trucks roaring down highways carrying things to us that we want and need. It has the meaning we see only when we are cold or hungry or out of work — the meaning we do not see when we are it. It has only the meaning we cannot see because it is still all around us. We are hungry only when we are not fed, and this is the meaning of the second question: We can only imagine living without oil. We cannot see it. We can only know its meaning through nondimensional experience. And when we have removed our own interest from imagining the meaning of oil, there will be a great understanding of who we are on the earth.

THE EARTH IS TOO SMALL FOR US AND FOR THE SUN THAT WE NEED. TO COVER great deserts and oceans would destroy habitat and ruin the weather. Trees and birds and children need sun to play in; we cannot take sunlight from them and from plants. This is the right answer to the wrong question. There is not enough Earth for the sun that we need. There is not even enough Earth. There will be pain and doing without what we want. There will be waiting to go places and riding with people we do not know. There will be longing for what we now have. And we may fail. We may run out before becoming what we are meant to be. Oil is energy only; we provide the order. But the sun shines on, and like a seed sprouting in the soil, we will grow toward it. We will build stems and leaves and grow toward the sun. We will use the oil that is here to become what we cannot be without it, that we may be without it when it no longer is.

Myth is who we think we are, that we may do.

Chapter 11

Becoming

The Land Between the Rivers

THERE ARE MANY IDEAS AS TO HOW CIVILIZATION GOT STARTED. IT MIGHT HAVE been a drought, a gradual change in temperature, or a need to band together for common defense. Many scholars think there had to have been a life-or-death challenge of some sort to have caused so great a leap in the intensity of human organization. The crisis came and went, but the organization remained, and went on to serve other purposes. But whatever the immediate cause, the beginning of civilization had to do with finding a steady and reliable food supply for a concentration of people.

Hunting and gathering or upland agronomy supports only small, temporary settlements. Herds move on, pasture and croplands wear out, and people find themselves on the move every few years. But on the floodplains of a major river, much more food can be grown in less space. The soil is deeper and richer, and if the river floods fairly regularly and not severely, the fertility of the soil is continually replenished. The same land can be used over again every year, and enough food can be grown to have some left over at the end of the year. People do not have to move on to new farmland. Permanent settlements with many people become practical, and a food surplus becomes possible, which means that there can be some people in the community who do not farm. They can build walls, make pottery and tools, keep the gods happy, and defend the homeland while still having something to eat. That is how civilization got started. The climate did change, neighbors did invade, but the advantage was always with the people who had a floodplain and a surplus and an organization to take advantage of the situation.

But you can't start a civilization by yourself. You need to work it out with other people. Floodplains produce a surplus of weeds and vines and bushes that have to be chopped out and cleared before the land is useful for farming. Fertility works against you at first. A tremendous amount of work goes into digging irrigation and drainage canals — work that takes a lot of people moving in the same general direction. It requires vision, initiative, cooperation, and organization to make it happen. The river must be tamed and harnessed so as to release its nourishment in a timely fashion, and so as not to destroy crops and homes. Every year new lands must be cleared, new ditches dug, levees constructed, and existing ditches cleared and repaired. It is not the kind of thing you can do on your own. You and your neighbors have to be convinced that you are better off in the long run by working very hard now, cutting and digging and scratching for the possibility of more food later. The work is not directly related to feeding your family now, so you will have to be fed in the short term by the system, by the surplus. You have to believe that the system will take care of you. You will have to be telling yourself something as you chop through the mud.

Who gives you the food? Where does it come from? Where does the food that you and your friends produce go? Who controls the surplus? Who keeps track of things? What if you don't like the system?

Writing is what holds it all together: writing and mythology. Writing keeps track of things by putting human thought and word into material form. If you say something with your mouth, it goes away as soon as you say it, but if you write it down, you will remember, and so will everyone else. You can show it again later. Writing is a particular order of things that stands for thought: little marks made with a stick on a mud tablet that you leave in the sun to dry. Little marks that mean anything you can say out loud, like So-and-so bought five measures of barley from So-and-so, and still owes payment for half, or So-and-so now owns such-and-such a field next to So-and-so's house. Writing is human thought extended into space and time. It is what keeps the system together, and, incidentally, what starts history. Civilization means buildings and art and surpluses and division of labor, and a humanity elevated some-what above the beasts of the field: All of these come with writing. Writing is the beginning of us, how we became a wholeness. Nothing really happened to us before writing.

In the beginning, it was the air-god, Enlil, who created the land between the rivers. Heaven and Earth were originally one. He divided Heaven, his father, from Earth, his mother, creating himself in the process.

> The lord, that which is appropriate verily he caused to appear,
> The lord whose decisions are unalterable,
> Enlil, who brings up the seed of the land from the earth,
> Took care to move away heaven from earth,
> Took care to move away earth from heaven,

In order to make grow the creature which came forth,
In the "bond of heaven and earth" (Nippur) he stretched out the...[6]

It was Enlil who gave you the pickax:

He brought the pickax into existence, the "day" came forth,
He introduced labor, decreed the fate,
Upon the pickax and basket he directs the "power."
Enlil made his pickax exalted,
His pickax of gold, whose head is of lapis lazuli,
The pickax of his house, of ... silver and gold,
His pickax whose ... is of lapis lazuli,
Whose tooth is a one-horned ox ascending a large wall.

The lord called up the pickax, decrees its fate,
He set the kindu, the holy crown, upon his head,
The head of man he placed in the mould,
Before Enlil he (man?) covers his land,
Upon his black-headed people he looked steadfastly.
The Anunnaki who stood about him,
He placed it (the pickax?) as a gift in their hands,
They soothe Enlil with prayer,
They give the pickax to the black-headed people to hold.

The pickax and the basket build cities,
The steadfast house the pickax builds, the steadfast house the pickax establishes,
The steadfast house it causes to prosper.

The house which rebels against the king,
The house which is not submissive to its king,
The pickax makes it submissive to the king.

Of the bad ... plants it crushes the head,
Plucks at the roots, tears at the crown,
The pickax spares the ... plants;
The pickax, its fate decreed by father Enlil,
The pickax is exalted.[7]

Enki, son of Enlil and god of the river, brought fertility and abundance to the floodplains and appointed an assistant to supervise irrigation works:

The plow and the yoke he directed,
The great prince Enki caused the ... ox to ...;
To the pure crops he roared,
In the steadfast field he made grain grow;
The lord, the jewel and ornament of the plain,
The ... farmer of Enlil,
Enkimdu, him of the canals and ditches,
Enki placed in their charge.

> The lord called to the steadfast field, he caused it to produce much grain,
> Enki made it bring forth its small and large beans ...,
> The ... grains he heaped up for the granary,
> Enki added granary to granary,
> With Enlil he increases abundance in the land ...[8]

In the right proportions and in the right places, Enki brought life to the cities of the floodplain. He was descended from the formless, timeless primeval sea from which all things are created, and to which all things may revert. Nammu, goddess of the primeval waters, was his mother. One day Enki was asleep in the deep. The lesser gods, the Anunnaki, were having trouble finding food and were complaining to Nammu. She woke Enki, saying:

> "O my son, rise from thy bed, from thy ... work what is wise,
> Fashion servants of the gods, may they produce their..."

Enki responded:

> O my mother, the creature whose name thou hast uttered, it exists,
>   Bind upon it the ... of the gods;
> Mix the heart of the clay that is over the abyss,
> The good and princely fashioners will thicken the clay,
>   Thou, do thou bring the limbs into existence;
> Ninmah (the earth-mother goddess) will work above thee,
> ... (goddess of birth) will stand by thee at thy fashioning;
> O my mother, decree thou its (the new born's) fate,
>   Ninmad will bind upon it the ... of the gods,
>   ... as man...[9]

You are created to work in the fields and feed the gods. The granary is at the temple.

> They (the Anunnaki) knew not the eating of bread,
> Knew not the dressing of garments,
> Ate plants with their mouth like sheep,
> Drank water from the ditch.

> In those days, in the creation chamber of the gods,
> In their house Dulkug, Lahar and Ashnan were fashioned;
> The produce of Lahar and Ashnan,
> The Anunnaki of the Dulkug drink, but remain unsated;
> For the sake of the good things in their pure sheepfolds,
> Man was given breath.[10]

You are here to bring grain to the temple. That is how it works, and it is true. Everything and everyone has its place. It is there to be seen, in the world all around you, but you have to look to see it. If it were not, it would not be on the tablets. Enlil gave you the pickax. He is still there in his wholeness, though we no longer see him for the parts. He is all around us, and too close to see.

Mythology is like money. It is true because everybody believes in it. It is so true that nobody ever thinks to question it. If we all wake up tomorrow morning and decide that all the pieces of paper in our pockets and all the numbers on our bank statements are really just pieces of paper and numbers, there will no longer be such a thing as money.

Enlil and Enki give us a place between the rivers, but it is a small place. We are here to feed the gods in the temple and take whatever fate they throw our way. If they decide to dry up the river, or cause our enemies to attack us, that is what we must live with. If the river washes away our crops and our houses, it is just something the gods felt like doing. Maybe we made them mad, or maybe they were not thinking about us. We have little control beyond begging and pleading for attention. We are a very small part of the big picture. But the part we are makes sense of what we do.

How could we imagine, then, what we have become? Shopping centers, aircraft carriers, tape recorders, Internet servers, subway trestles: How could we have known that it was all in the floodplains? What was the intention, or was there any? Civilization is what we did, and then what we became. It is the order in what we do together.

The Ball in Space

SOME YEARS LATER, THE PLACE BECAME LARGER AND MORE CENTRALLY LOCATED. We became above and apart from nature. We were subject to the will of God, as before, but He was more directly interested in what we were doing. He made us the crown jewel of His creation, the center of His universe. He made it for us to live in and lord over. The earth and the stars and the plants and fishes in the sea were a backdrop for the unfolding drama of the human struggle against the forces of evil.

Everything revolved around us. Everything happened down here, at center stage. But there was a continuous state of unsettledness. Things were never completely resolved. The chosen mixed with the unchosen, the good with the evil, the Air with Earth and Water. It was not always clear where one began and another ended. There was a natural place for everything: the earth at the center of the universe, the spheres of Water and Air around Earth, and Fire beyond them, but the spheres often overlapped. They were often muddied by the imperfections of life in this world. Events were uncertain, and thereby dramatic. If the universe were perfect, we could not do things, and we would not be human.

Perfection was up above Earth, and above Water, Air, and Fire. The spheres of the moon, sun, planets, and stars were not of the terrestrial elements, but of a heavenly, weightless, quintessential substance. They were beyond all but the remotest human contemplation. There was no strife there, no doing. God lived there, in the perfection of being, looking down on us and judging what we did. He gave us what we needed and gave us clear directions, and caused all earthly objects to seek the center of the universe. This is how He kept order. If we did not stop it, a stone would fall down through Air or Water. He caused Air to seek its place above Earth, and above Water, and He caused the Fire to leap up through Air. If left to themselves, the elements would work themselves into their circles of perfection, the circle being God's manifestation of perfection. But we do not leave things to themselves. We do things. God loves us anyway, and wants us to be perfect against our inner nature.

We knew this was the way things were because we could see it. The sun and moon moved around the earth, and the planets orbited slowly through the heavens in perfect arcs across the night sky. You did not have to have any special knowledge to see it. Everything down here was a mixture of the four earthly elements, some combination of solid, liquid, gas, and energy. These constituted all things; there were no other substances in this world, and there were no more fundamental substances to which they could be reduced. God made them as they were. Things fall to the ground by the degree of their baseness; earthly objects like rocks and cannon balls fall hardest because they seek their natural place in the universe. They seek not the center of the earth, but the center of the universe, which is also the center of the earth.

This was a great wholeness, and a great beauty. It explained what we saw and what we were doing, and our place in the larger picture of things. There was certainly no reason to change it. It was not a theory or a model, but reality — not a view of the world, but the world itself. There was nothing else that could be. It was so powerful a picture of universal order that it remained alive and well for more than a century after it was known to be false.

What kept the Earth-centered universe alive for so long after its deathblow was the fear of seeing something that was not in it. Nobody wanted to see anything that was not in it. The consequences were too great. There was an organized effort to keep the universe as it was, despite whatever might be noticed to the contrary. Things that did not fit were ignored or explained away. New theories were developed by scientists of the time, but they were always within the confines of the prevailing mythology: *The earth had to be kept in its proper relation to the heavens.* Scientists liked to feel that what they were looking at was real, and they did not like to get tangled up in metaphysics. It was better to leave the metaphysics up to the metaphysicians and get back to work. Fundamental concepts, therefore, were not questioned, and only certain answers were allowable. Nobody wanted to destroy the world and construct a new one. It was much easier to "shoehorn" enigmatic observations into mythologically acceptable concepts. The shoehorns came in the form of "epicycles."

Observers had noticed since ancient times that the outer planets — Mars, Jupiter, and Saturn — did not move in perfectly circular orbits around the earth. They moved forward at first, and then *backward* for a while, before continuing forward again. This "retrograde motion" was deeply disturbing to everyone who understood it because it indicated that there was something uncircular, and therefore imperfect, about the quintessential realm. God was doing something very ungodly. How can He allow a heavenly body to move so erratically? A mythologically correct concept had to be found to explain what was seen. The answer was the "epicycle," or a small circular path within the larger circular path — a detour, but a circular detour. Retrograde motion was just a twirling about of the outer planets, a little curlicue ornamentation of an overall orbital motion around the earth. The epicycle was a complication, true, and an assumption, but it kept the world in one piece and the big picture whole. God's purpose in ornamenting an already perfect motion was questionable, but the style of the workmanship was distinctly His own.

The sun and moon still orbited perfectly, as did the fixed stars in the heavens beyond. Only retrograde motion needed to be shoehorned into the obviously true picture of things. It was still a perfect, whole, and a beautiful overview of reality the way it really was. Everything fit. Epicycles were a necessary assumption, something that had to be true. An entire universe would not collapse for the sake of a few tiny points of light in the night sky.

But more observations, and more careful and systematic observations, led to more and more epicycles. A single epicycle within the larger orbital motion was not enough to explain new studies done on the motions of the outer planets. There had to be an epicycle within the epicycle, and another one within that one. They were all circles, and therefore perfect and Godly, but the picture they drew was no longer simple, and no longer beautiful. The music of the spheres was lost in a din of moving parts, and the poem of creation hidden in a tangle of footnotes and parentheses. The shoe no longer fit. But the Earth-centered universe lived on because it had to.

Nicolaus Copernicus (1473–1543) came up with an understanding of planetary motion that was mathematically simpler than the Earth-centered universe. It was difficult to picture visually, it collided head-on with the mythology of the times, and it violated common sense, but it was simpler — not simpler to understand, just simpler, and more beautiful. The only reason we like it now is that it is simpler. (If you do not mind complication, you can still get the Earth-centered universe to work even now.) Copernicus's idea did not change anything about what was observed, only the point of view from which it was observed. It did not change the facts, only the understanding of the facts, and thereby the understander. It did not change the universe; it changed us.

The word *planet* means "wandering star." It was noticed from ancient times that almost all the stars stay "fixed," and only a few move from night to night. Copernicus said that we are one of those that moves. The earth is a point of light wandering about in the sky like Venus or Jupiter. But whose sky? How do we *see* the earth this way? Why would things fall to the earth if the center of the universe were somewhere else? Where *is* the center of the universe? Why do I not feel that I am moving? Why do buildings and mountains not tumble to the ground as the earth swerves around the sun? Where is heaven? Where is God? What is "up"?

Copernicus knew that his idea was absurd. He had no proof that it was true and there was no way to begin to answer the questions that it raised. There was no explanation for *why* the planets might move around the sun, no known law or force that would keep them in their orbits, no physics to support his idea, and certainly no metaphysics. There was no such thing as a telescope. There was no way to detect the "stellar parallax," or the slight difference in the positions of stars every six months that would have to be apparent if the earth moved around the sun once a year. All he had was a simpler idea, and a more beautiful one. But it was mythologically incorrect. The Church would get him. Copernicus knew this, and did not allow his idea to be published until shortly before his death. It was more than a hundred years later before the idea was generally accepted. Galileo was arrested for believing it.

We all believe it now because we are told it is true. We see pictures of the solar system in science textbooks with the sun in the center and the nine planets, including the earth, circling in their orbits, but this is not what we see in the world. The sun still "rises" in the morning and "sets" at night. The planets are still points of light in the night sky. Everything looks as it did to the ancient Babylonians. The only difference is us. "We" are more the "looking at the textbook picture" than the "looking at the sky." We are the experience of many people and not our own directly. If we had to see ourselves standing on a ball hurling through space at many thousands of miles per hour before believing it, we would not be able to be what we now are. Reality is what we experience through others, and we are that experience. We do not see it, only envision it. We believe what they tell us, and it is true. We would see it, too, were we in their place.

The idea of the earth in space has relieved us of the need to verify physical reality with direct perceptual experience. We have to trust what we are told. If anyone were to take the trouble to look through the telescopes for himself, and check the figures and brush up on astrophysics, he would come to the same conclusions that are presented in the textbooks. Or we believe that he would. We believe it the way we believe there is gold in Fort Knox. We do not think about it, we just believe it, and that is the structure of consciousness that makes us who we are now.

The Unenclosed Circle

NEWTONIAN MECHANICS MADE THE COPERNICAN IDEA PHYSICALLY PLAUSIBLE. Tycho Brahe (1546–1601) made the observations, and Johann Kepler (1571–1630) came up with the formulas, but it was Sir Isaac Newton (1642–1727) who first showed why the planets move they way they do. They are subject, he said, to the same physical laws as apply on Earth. Physics up there is the same as physics down here; the same force that makes an apple fall from a tree makes a planet follow an elliptical orbit around the sun. He did not know what the force was, or how it could work, only that it is the same in both worlds, and that, by implication, there is really only one world subject to the same set of universal physical laws. Things work in heaven the way they do on Earth.

And it is a material world. It exists whether we are looking at it or not. It is logical, rational, and predictable. We can tell exactly where Venus and Mars will be two hundred years from now because we can measure their motions and we know the physical laws to which they are subject. If our predictions are a little off it is only because our knowledge is imperfect. If we could know everything there is to know about every object in the universe, we could tell where they all were at anytime in the past and where they will be at anytime in the future. Our knowledge will never be that good, but in theory, it could be. We may not know everything, but everything is knowable. The entire universe receives the imprint of human thought, and the possibility of human doing. We can go there and move something around. Heaven and Earth are no longer in their proper places. The metaphysical conjugation of heaven and Earth brings the imperfection of human doing into outer space and, at the same time, the quintessential perfectibility of man to Earth. Man is not God but he is like God. People have the right to do anything with the earth that they have the capacity do, and there is no stopping us now. The process is irreversible. We might not get it right, but there is nothing in principle to keep us from trying. We can do now what only God could do before.

It is frightening to consider. For two million years we were animals who stood up. For five thousand years, we were cities of mud and stone. For ten generations we have been mechanized industry. Now, in the present generation, we are electronic circuitry. It is not change we are becoming but accelerated change. The rate of change is changing. We are becoming something else at an exponential rate. We are not people inventing things to make our lives easier; we are a new and burgeoning form of life, sprouting in all directions, gorging resources, overflowing and outgrowing ourselves. We are not human; we are something that has humans and machines and computers in it.

Our hands cut weeds with the pickax, plant wheat and barley, bring water through fields and cities, break rocks, and melt them to metal. Our arms, with the power of machinery, turn ore and fiber to clothing, transportation, and shelter. Our fingers send electrons pulsing through copper at the speed of light to make ideas, language, and pictures of distant lands. We secrete rivers of steel and concrete. Water flows from underground pipes through houses and bodies, and back out to unknown places. Food comes in clear plastic vacuoles. Wires stretch overhead. Membranes of wood and concrete surround us, the air within specially prepared. Buildings breathe in and out. Factories and switchboards and houses are what we are. We move in sealed capsules through broad streaming arteries, over bridges and under rivers, pulsing in and out of towns in fixed rhythm. Rails cross plains and valleys to great clusters of buildings. We look through cathode ray tubes to times and places our bodies do not occupy. Electromagnetic images crowd the airways, passing from carbon to silicon and back to carbon. We think with computers.

All of this was to make us richer and more civilized, but still who we were. It was to be separate from us — dead, inanimate material, sitting out there waiting to be used. It was not to move but by us. We were to be each in our own piece of space, and of time, separate from what we had made, and from each other. Space was the separation, and not the wholeness.

The wholeness is around curvatures of space and time, and through spaces between them. It is what space is in.

ALL IS BEFORE US. EACH IN OUR OWN BODY FEELS THE WHOLENESS IN THE ORDER of what is felt. It is all there is. We hear it touching in the call of wild birds or in the roar of a highway. We see it, watching thoughts and dreams. We see it sitting still, high on a mountaintop. The universe of space unfolds in the touch of light.

WE ARE THE HUMAN PART OF US. IN THIS GENERATION OUR NUMBERS HAVE doubled. Nonhumans are dying. Holes appear in the ozone. The atmosphere shifts to carbon, and the weather changes. Resources are consumed. It cannot go on because there will be no resources when they are gone. Governments make bombs and tanks instead of schools and hospitals. Everybody dies in the next major war. Hunger increases; farmland decreases. People move to cities and find nothing. Species disappear, forests burn, the coral dies in the oceans. The rate increases because of what we are doing. We keep doing it because we do not know what else to do. We do not know what else to do because we do not know what we are.

What we have become cannot be said or pointed to. It is not a shape, or a thing in the box. It is a relation to the weather and to what we feel at the bottom of our feet. It is a wholeness that includes the beholder. That is why we feel drawn to rivers and tall buildings and why wild places do not have to be seen. Wild places are not in places that are seen. It is why a thunderstorm or a great tree stops us in time. We will not grasp it; it is not there. It is wolves and owls and whales. Our ancestors knew it as spirit. They knew it, and knew who they were, even if it was wrong. They knew themselves in relation to the earth and sky. We are who they were before they gave way to a bigger place, for us. We have grown too big even for it.

When we are ancestors, our children will live in enclosures with Air and plants we found between the rivers. Earth will come with them wherever they go. They will be sealed inside, at one with soil, Water, circuits, and bacteria. They will spread foliage to the sun and to other suns. Gravity will be a selection. The structure of consciousness will change. When the separation is forgotten, the task of being human will end.

The ball in space will be an unenclosed circle: the place to breathe outside, where plants grow in open air and the sun shines directly, where soil is still dirt. Its openness now is our separation from it. It will be the sacred place that it is, the husk from which we emerge. We should keep it. Its oceans are our blood. We should keep it to know ourselves through time.

NATURE HAS BEEN BIG ENOUGH TO ABSORB OUR QUARRELS AND MISTAKES, BUT now we are growing too fast and must set out on our own. We have to leave. The seed is cracked and swollen, enzymes melt rocks and mountains, and there is no turning back. We have to grow toward the light or die. There is enough iron ore in the body of the earth, and enough Air and coal and manganese and oil, exactly enough. If it were a human thing, we would call it a plan.

Thank you.

Chapter 12

Being and Doing

OR IT MAY BE THAT THERE ARE OTHERS, AND THAT OURS HAS FALLEN ON ROCKY ground, or that there are none. It does not matter.

Endnotes

1 Berkeley, George, "The Third Dialogue," Three Dialogues Between Hylas and Philonous, in *A New Theory of Vision and Other Writings*, introduction by A. D. Lindsay, Everyman's Library, (New York: E.P. Dutton, 1910, p. 287).

2 Ibid., pp. 235–238.

3 By Einstein's Principle of Equivalence, a gravitational field is the same thing, physically, as acceleration. Earth's gravitational field is a fixed rotation of space–time into the mass dimension, and that is why you always feel the earth pushing up through your shoes.

For those who care to think of such things, a *linear* acceleration is an interchange of one space for two time dimensions, while an *angular* acceleration (say, going around a curve) is an interchange of two spaces for one time dimension. Both involve the mass dimension and are "felt" throughout the body as the g force.

4 Copyright 1984 by John McCutcheon/Appalsongs (ASCAP). From the CD "Winter Solstice" (Cambridge, Mass.: Rounder Records, 1984). Reprinted by permission.

5 These and other figures in the section are estimates from Ayres, Ed, *God's Last Offer* (New York: Four Walls, Eight Windows, 1999).

6 Kramer, Samuel Noah, *Sumerian Mythology* (New York: Harper & Row), p. 52. Copyright 1961 by Samuel Noah Kramer. Originally published in 1944 by the American Philosophical Society and used here by permission from the American Philosophical Society.

7 Ibid., pp. 52,53.

8 Ibid., p. 61.

9 Ibid., p. 70.

10 Ibid., p. 73.

Printed in the United States
87853LV00002B/34/A